T0246483

JEREMIAD

MIROLAND IMPRINT 45

Canada Council   Conseil des Arts
for the Arts   du Canada

ONTARIO ARTS COUNCIL
CONSEIL DES ARTS DE L'ONTARIO

an Ontario government agency
un organisme du gouvernement de l'Ont

Canadä

Guernica Editions Inc. acknowledges the support of the Canada Council
for the Arts and the Ontario Arts Council. The Ontario Arts Council
is an agency of the Government of Ontario.

We acknowledge the financial support of the Government of Canada.

ISTVAN KANTOR

JEREMIAD

MiroLand
p u b l i s h e r s

(GUERNICA)
TORONTO—CHICAGO—BUFFALO—LANCASTER (U.K.)
2023

Guernica Founder: Antonio D'Alfonso

Michael Mirolla, editor
Cover design and interior design: Errol F. Richardson
Guernica Editions Inc.
287 Templemead Drive, Hamilton, ON L8W 2W4
2250 Military Road, Tonawanda, N.Y. 14150-6000 U.S.A.
www.guernicaeditions.com

Distributors:
Independent Publishers Group (IPG)
600 North Pulaski Road, Chicago IL 60624
University of Toronto Press Distribution (UTP)
5201 Dufferin Street, Toronto (ON), Canada M3H 5T8

First edition.
Printed in Canada.

Legal Deposit—Third Quarter
Library of Congress Catalog Card Number: 2023936336
Library and Archives Canada Cataloguing in Publication
Title: Jeremiad / Istvan Kantor.
Names: Kantor, Istvan, author.
Identifiers: Canadiana 20230439829 | ISBN 9781771838306 (softcover)
Classification: LCC PS8621.A595 J47 2023 | DDC 818/.6—dc23

CONTENTS

BEYOND THE POWER OF WORDS
INTRODUCTION BY EWAN WHYTE

THE ACT OF REBELLION is a form of creation for Istvan Kantor. His art interventions have made him both famous and infamous in the art world and beyond. He started his Blood Campaign in 1979 in Montreal, spreading Neoist manifestos against art institutions, museums and corporate interests (and provoking harsh reactions). In one of his interventions he purposefully made a large blood-X by splashing his own blood on the wall between two Picasso paintings, at the Museum of Modern Art in New York. He waited for the police with the intention of getting arrested so he could tell his motives directly to the judges and thus, through the media, to the public. He was charged with causing $10 million in damages, a felony, but after two and a half years of court battles he managed to reduce charges to a misdemeanor, with a fine and avoiding prison. Stubborn and uncompromising, Kantor continued his Blood Campaign at different locations in Canada, the USA and Europe. He was subsequently arrested again and banned from most of the major art galleries and museums of the world. It is interesting to note that Kantor's art actions are often the initial impulses and/or the source material for his literary works, including biographic novels, manifestoes, essays, scripts, and poetry. A selection of them constitute part of this book, the first major publication of his writings in Canada, properly entitled *Jeremiad*.

Sometime in May/1979 Kantor came up with an idea and went to the street to "start something new" carrying a chair and a Neoism sign. At a street corner in downtown Montreal he attached the Neoism sign to the back of the chair and sat down. When passers-by stopped and asked him what is Neoism he boldly replied: "I have no idea. That's why I'm sitting here to find out what it is." His simple street action triggered immediate interest and generated conversations about the idea of Neoism, only a name without content. What Kantor basically proposed was to create a collective response to a philosophical question that had no historical background in order to start a world-wide art movement. And it worked! He initiated a process that within a short time became the subject matter of provocative art events and academic debates.

What is Neoism? It is anti-authoritarian and anti-institutional but ultimately the definition of Neoism is that it has no definition and that everyone can define Neoism the way they want to define it. It also can be engaging, riotous, funny, ironic, self-satirical, and poetic nonsense. It has been the central focus of Kantor's creative output for the last 40 plus years and continues today. His bible size credo *The Book of Neoism?!* is the result of several decades of conceiving, accumulating definitions of Neoism through extensive plundering of ideas from writers, philosophers, artists, scientists, revolutionaries, historians, factory workers, athletes and beggars. It was first published in 2018 by *paranoia publishing* in Tallinn, Estonia and reissued in 2022 by *Autonomedia* in New York.

Although Kantor is mostly known as a performance artist, he started out writing songs and poetry. He read classic Hungarian literature extensively in his youth. He also learned to compose folk and popular music as well. He has retained a poetic way of seeing in his work.

The very act or gesture of rebelling is elemental and is relatable to everyone. It also tends to strongly connect with each new underground arts generation encountering Neoism. Kantor's performances of rebellion are a fragmentation of something primal in all of us. It is as if they are near what Northrop Frye called "hieroglyphic stage art" in ancient imaginations, languages and cultures (but is still poking around in limited doses today). An example of this is Homeric poetry, where the name for the sky is also the god itself. In using this kind of imagination or metonymic way of seeing the world we are brought into a numinous way of seeing. We are hard wired to relate to this way of perceiving, as we have lived for thousands of years with this way of seeing, both outside ourselves and within (though we, according to Frye, are in a Demotic age of imagination, which tends to put us deliberately at odds with this richer hard-wired mythical-numinous way of perceiving, while unconsciously craving it).

Kantor incorporates aspects of this in some of his performances and brings it to us with humour. One of his pranks is to divide the audience into two groups, artists and spectators or revolutionaries and executioners who pretend to kill each other by mimicking machine gun sounds through their voices. This audience engagement puts him on another level of surprise, and dark humour.

Kantor's use of his own blood in his performances is immediate. He does this professionally, by putting a tourniquet around his arm, and then proceeds to draw his own blood with a needle in open view. One time he did this while slowly swinging upside-down on a trapeze in an art gallery on Queen Street in Toronto. The effect is intimate. It is elemental. We all know blood is instrumental in life itself and this life essence we all have is being dripped on canvases or painted with or used as a pendulum dripping pattern on the floor. This is an experience of a reminder of death and a bringing us to an earthy understanding of it when we smell the blood.

It reminds me of the once famous book *The Denial of Death* by Ernest Becker. In Becker's book there are lists of mundane things that are unconscious daily reminders of death, a universal one for example is going to the toilet. In it, like in Mircea Eliade's The sacred and the Profane, where daily mystical things the most diehard atheists are shown to unintentionally engage in daily. We understand these things; death and Mysticism are unconsciously around us all the time.

Istvan Kantor's performances with blood are a reminder, a celebration and a denial of death. They are also a reminder of fragility and violence being a constant on-tap possibility. A large part of Kantor's work is expressed through intuition, instinct, where the unconscious adds to conscious intent. That's what exactly triggered his creative interest to start making art, writing poetry and songs at an early stage of his life, living in Budapest, Hungary. Perhaps it's relevant to mention that his backgrounds include working as paramedic nurse and studying at medical university.

The roots of Kantor's feelings towards authority were defined early in his life as a child growing up during the 1956 Hungarian Revolution. His childhood experience had a very deep impact on him as a 7 years old and it turned into a lifelong motivation for his creative ambitions, as a creator and thinker, retraceable almost all of his writings and art works:

So it was a very beautiful day and we were all in an air-raid shelter and there were bombs going off. You know it was a very exciting time. And I somehow got out from the air-raid shelter before my parents or anyone else, there were lots of people in the air-raid shelter, could see. There were lots of people in the shelter and it was very small. So I went towards the street, and I had my little toy gun which my grandfather made for me from wood. I went behind a tree, but I didn't hide well enough and I pointed my gun to the first tank, and they saw me. Because at that time the Russians were afraid of the little kids because they would throw Molotov Cocktails at the tanks, and lots of people died, even the little kids because they blew up together with the tanks, so they stopped and a soldier jumped out from the first tank of the convoy and came towards me making a motion to come and saying 'idi suda' come here in Russian. And then I ran back to the building and hid there. The Russians surrounded the building and said they were looking for the little boy with the gun. Fortunately the janitor spoke Russian and was smart enough to say something to the soldiers and after a while they just left. Maybe they didn't have time for that, a little boy with a toy gun. But the people in the air-raid shelter they broke my little gun like in a ritual. And they were very upset at my grandfather that he made me this thing. But it was very interesting because this was a kind of oppression that was happening at that time, they lived in fear. So what I created was something what they didn't want which I repeated many times afterwards, that's how I grew up creating conflicts.

For the next two decades he lived in an oppressive, totalitarian society under the Warsaw Pact's double standards. At first it was most noticeable for him by the carefully censured education in school. This is what inflamed the source of his rebelliousness. Kantor's first and main escape from being brainwashed by the oppressive environment of Communism was reading and writing. He read and first started to write poetry, mostly under the influence of the great classic and contemporary Hungarian poets/writers, especially Endre Ady, but also the international avant-garde, mostly French, Russian and American writers. Poetry was his main expression for the first two decades of his life, especially inspired by the Beat Generation poets, and though he went through changes and got involved with different forms of art and expression, it remained his inspirational source and a driving force in his outlook on the world.

Under both oppressive forces, the dictatorial political rules of the country and the dictatorial rules of his father at home, Kantor struggled throughout his youth to break out and be himself. He was always stopped by circumstances in whatever he tried to accomplish. He wrote his own folk songs and performed them accompanied by his guitar in clubs and youth camps, travelling around the country like a Hungarian Bob Dylan. He wrote lyrics for rock bands, had his own folk band and explored a new form of lyrics based on ready-made material, like newspaper articles, letters, books of law, folk ballads and matchbox covers. He created happenings, while also studying medical science. He even briefly worked as paramedic, but he always seemed to get into trouble. He was kicked out from cultural institutions, and eventually from University. He was investigated by both the police and the Communist political authorities. At this time, he had constant fights with his father. He lived the marginalized life of a young outsider, expelled from student clubs and even from his home. It was during this time, he would go to the countryside to have some sense of personal freedom.

In 1976 he finally fled to Paris where he started a new life. He was granted political refugee status and became a subway singer, making a menial living by playing his own folk songs while he learned French. A year later he immigrated to Montreal. By that time, through the mail art network, he was in contact with many artists around the world. Shortly after his arrival in Montreal he left for the USA to join David Zack in Portland, Oregon. Zack was a correspondence artist, poet and journalist whom Kantor met in Budapest at the Young Artists' Club, in April 1976 where Zack exhibited his mail art works and his show had a considerable impact on Kantor. He spent six months in Portland where he performed in galleries and clubs. He played improvised "syphon music," wrote new songs and poetry, and put out an underground record. Finally Kantor was doing what he always wanted to do in a completely new and free environment. He also changed his name to Monty Cantsin and became the main advocate of the "open-pop-star concept" he developed in collaboration with David Zack, and that eventually resulted as a principal idea for Neoism.

Kantor/Cantsin also travelled to San Francisco where he met some of the early beat poets, Lawrence Ferlinghetti, Allen Ginsberg, Gary Snyder, the young Jim Carroll and many others. Jack Kerouac, William Burroughs, Gregory Corso, Richard Brautigan ... and others had a significant influence on him. Leaving Portland Kantor returned to Montreal where he organized one of the largest ever Mail Art exhibitions under the title "BRAIN IN THE MAIL." It opened in February/1979 at Véhicule Art. At the same time Kantor formed a performance art group from local artists that became the base for Neoism, which he officially launched on May 22nd on a street corner in downtown Montreal, across the street from McGill University, at the corner of Sherbrooke and McGill streets.

It is less well known that Kantor is also a media artist. He has produced a large number of videos and super8 films. His robotic art works, sculptural machinery and most recent AI installations have been widely shown at new technology festivals, and digital-media exhibitions in Canada, USA, Europe and Asia. He is also a singer/songwriter, with a dozen albums to his name.

Kantor's body of work is substantial. This book is a selection of the range of his creative output. Performing and writing under different names, Istvan Kantor, Monty Cantsin, Amen, Esmeralda Eldorado, Sawang, Csö Kántor, he has presented his Neoist art performances, installations, poetry, manifestos, music, paintings, and sculptures in many countries and on all continents, creating collaborations and friendships with artists around the world.

Istvan Kantor is a recipient of the Governor General's Award of Canada for Visual and Media Arts. He tirelessly continues to create.

Portrait of Istvan Kantor

Photo Edward Gajdel 2010

SPECTACLE OF NOISE

IT WAS A LONG, depressing and very cold winter. I hadn't been outside for a long time. I survived on rice and water. I tried to save money by not heating and keeping the lights off. Gas and electricity rates were way too high. It was dark and freezing in my studio.

I rented the basement of a rundown warehouse building in the east end of Capital City. It was in bad shape but at least large enough and affordable. I was probably the last one living in an old-fashioned space like that. I loved the windowless darkness, the smell of ruins, the decadency of decay. I could spend hours looking at the stained, discoloured walls, the dripping ceiling, the rusty, corroded, broken heating and air conditioning systems.

Most of the old warehouses in downtown had been demolished and replaced by luxury condos. Those who couldn't afford the high rents were taken to concentration camps. I heard there were riots in the poor neighbourhoods. I hoped that soon there would be a revolution.

During the spring, when it got a bit warmer, I was ready again for exploration. I started the day with a heavy workout session followed by masturbation. I felt like a machine with no purpose. The most exciting idea I could think about was self-destruction. I wondered if it was possible to commit suicide through yoga meditation.

My favourite activity was to break into old, abandoned factories still waiting to be demolished. It was all about mortality and death in relation to architecture and sex. I climbed up to the roofs and looked down at the city while jumping, dancing around with my camera, doing convulsive movements, freely jerking my body, enjoying my alienation and loneliness. But I knew I wasn't exactly alone. I knew I was being watched by surveillance cameras, by a complete spy system built for monitoring individuals. Every individual was considered to be a potential terrorist. But I didn't really care. My own system of survival was much more important.

I chose the path of a life-long struggle to escape from the system of control. I searched for people with whom I could share my ideas and release the tension of my mind and body. I got drawn into obsessive relationships which increased my fascination with sex and convulsion.

I made plans to create a commune which would provide its members enough food, continuous entertainment and free sex, something like the hippies practiced in the 60s. Of course it was only utopian daydreaming without realistic basis. After a while I gave it up and focused on my own my individual autonomy.

The city was ruled under the dictatorship of the landlord's union and controlled by a robotic surveillance technology transmission network system. There was only one solution, I realized, only one possible way to go: to wipe out my memory, to delete my existence. The mission of self-annihilation, a form of self-induced lobotomy.

The city's law was programmed and enforced by the RST (Robotic Surveillance Transmission) under the leadership of GTN (Global Technology Network) sponsored by the ASRPA (Advanced Scientific Research Project Agency) of the RENTAGON. Individual units were monitored by a micro-electro-mechanical system, known as SMOKE (Surveillance Machinery for Optico-Kinetic Engineering), a hyper-intelligence technology based on the use of info-dust and data-smoke particles extended with ultra-miniature sensor-detectors. Those who couldn't afford the extremely high rents were taken to Fitness and Mental Care Rehabilitation Centres and from there they were transferred to Voluntary Labor Camps located in the central area of Capital City.

My only attachment to the scientific measure of the existing order of things was my association with Transmission Research Society. TRS tried to achieve its goal of self-induced datamorphose through telepathokinetic yoga meditation, repetitious mechanical exercise and trans-robotic machine-sex action. But above all I was determined to remove myself from the techno sphere of complete control and disappear like an abandoned body-machine with no purpose thrown into the corner of a junkyard.

Throughout the winter I only turned on the heat once in a while for a short time, for temporary relief of my misery. The heat was my drug. I stood in front of the gas blower and let the hot wind go through my body, warm up my bones and stimulate my mind. It was a trans-linear, hallucinatory experience. I can't tell which year it was. Through the grid of the heater I gazed into the past present and future simultaneously at once.

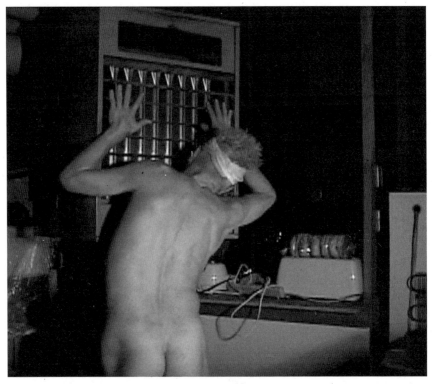

The heat was my drug

Photo self taken

FATHERLAND

MY CREATIVITY WAS SHAPED in the ruins. I was born in the post-war era in a land of devastation and hopeless misery. I grew up in a spooky world populated by dictators, rebels, traitors, assassins, police informers, double agents, second-hand dealers, knife-sharpeners, dogcatchers, and child molesters. My playgrounds were bombed-out buildings overgrown with weeds, and dark basements exhaling the stench of poverty. This decadent scene of decay, rubble, scrap, and junk produced the background for the Orwellian atmosphere of personality cult. It also provided a perfect feeding ground for rebellion.

I was part of the first generation communist youth, born into communism in 1949, in Budapest, Fatherland. In school we were educated to become militant communists. Our look and our intellect were produced by communist ideology. I liked the uniform, red tie, white shirt, badges, membership ID, the propaganda language and the gestures. I also enjoyed the ceremonies and celebrations, especially the anthem-like songs. I recited revolutionary poems at special events and regularly spoke on the school radio. I was selected to become a leader of my age group. We got trained in summer camps.

From a very early stage of my life, my father tried to persuade me to focus only on science, biology especially, and used all his efforts to convince me that becoming a doctor was my ultimate purpose in life. Perhaps he was mistaken by my strong attraction to nature revealed in childhood, collecting snakes and frogs, dissecting small dead birds, making skeletal models, stuffing and preserving specimens, regularly digging out human bones from abandoned cemeteries, and spending hours looking at microscopic things. My father rather encouraged me in these activities, and, in conclusion, decided that I was born to be a doctor.

Many years later when I was already a medical student, I often brought home all kinds of human organs. To the horror of my grandmother, our refrigerator was packed with human brains, long strings of the nervous system, testicles, human embryos. I could study them in the comfort of my own room and to show them to my friends. I wasn't against studying medical science and I cherished the possibility of becoming a research scientist, but I never had any intention to become a practicing doctor. And besides, I was also drawn to exploring my talents in many other fields: poetry, music, visual art, sports—they were all important for me. My father was frustrated and tried to stop me from doing what he considered to be unimportant and useless, but against his will I kept experimenting with radically different ideas.

"And, on the other hand, why can't I just become an apprentice in a factory and join the proletarians around the world?" I posed this rather philosophical question to myself in negation to my father's will, while also acknowledging the fact that, born into a middle-class, intellectual family, a choice like that couldn't be the apotheosis of my career. Many years later, after arriving in Montreal as a new immigrant, I worked as dishwasher, elevator boy and also got a job in a factory as machine operator. But, above all, from a young age, I was captivated by the lives of revolutionaries and I wanted to be one of them. Among my long list of idols were Che Guevara, Trotsky, Spartacus, Emilio Zapata, Bakunin, Emma Goldman; Hungarian poets Sándor Petőfi, Endre Ady, Tamkó Sirató Károly; artists Kazimir Malevitch, André Breton, Alfred Jarry, to only mention a few. When my father ripped off my Guevara poster hanging on the wall of my small room at our summer house in Surány and threw it into the garbage, it didn't solve anything but only increased the never-ending, lifelong conflicts between us.

We had an old gramophone in our living room and, starting at age 7 or 8, my sister Kati and I listened to all of the old 78rpm Bakelite records from my grandfather's eclectic collection—classical, folk, and popular music. We loved the popular old songs from pre-WW2—1920s and 30s—and learned almost all of them by heart. We often performed them *a cappella* at family events and I also entertained my school friends with my own solo interpretations. I also loved the anthem-like workman songs, the revolutionary marches, the hymnic songs of communism commemorating the heroic struggle of the people. We learned them in school and performed them at celebratory events such as the Workers' Day Parade on May 1st. They became deeply engraved in my heart and memory. Experimenting with the form of the song as a highly creative art-product became my lifelong interest.

My father was highly-educated, a university professor, an academic, and, at home, an incorrigible tyrannical ruler. He was an autocrat who lived under the constant pressure of a political system but he never joined the Communist Party. His professional knowledge and skills successfully kept him in respected positions. My love and respect for him often turned into hate. Each time one of my school teachers came to our house to advise him that I had talents in acting, music, or sports, he politely kicked them out and told them to never bother again. He really tried to protect me not only from outside influences but also from myself. He decided that my sister, Kati, should take piano lessons, which she did, but hated them and dropped out. Meanwhile I, who really wanted to learn music, wasn't allowed. I learned to play the guitar on my own with help from friends and I was already 18 when I secretly took piano lessons.

My father's dictatorial ways governed our childhood and school years, ruptured by our occasional refusal to obey his orders, which he punished with physical violence using his leather belt, while my mother kept menacing us all that she'd jump out from the balcony. My mom's desperate attempts to make us kids conduct ourselves properly and to control my father's violence were almost always ineffectual, short-lived outbursts of her wounded emotions. Her dream to have a university education was toppled by the war and her marriage to my father at the age of 20. She gradually transformed into a repressed housewife so typical in conservative families ruled by authoritarian husbands. Guided by self-sacrifice, she took care of all the labour at home, including cleaning, shopping, washing, and ironing.

Cooking and baking were carried out by my gramma, a highly creative family force. She was a skilled painter of landscape and still life, abruptly stopped in her artist career under the pressures of social circumstances. As a grandmother she spent her long life mostly in the kitchen nourishing us with a large variety of tasty and healthy meals. I loved watching her operating a Singer sewing machine and listening to the mechanical noise of the wheels. The hypnotic monotony and her coordinated arm and leg movements made my mind swirl away into a land of fantasy but when I suddenly woke up I never remembered anything. No celestial lights or sparkling mountains, no friendly giants or flying chocolate cakes, no supernatural singing ghosts ... but through the windows I heard my friends' voices calling me from the street and I ran down to join them.

We lived in a central neighbourhood of Budapest, in an apartment building populated by a wide diversity of residents with very different jobs and identities: intellectuals, factory workers, hardcore government officials, militant communists, old-fashioned craftsmen, people with disabilities and lots of kids of the same age. I liked to visit our neighbours regardless of their social status. I was the darling of everyone. It was almost like a utopian community; everybody knew each other.

Around age 13, I got my own room right next to the kitchen, which used to be the maid's room in previous times, before communism. It was small but for me it seemed immense, my own room where finally I could officially declare my independence, read my favourite books, play guitar, write poetry and songs. I finished my homework fast enough by early afternoon and hung out with my neighbourhood clan of disobedient kids hosting serious gang fights almost every day among the ruins of wars and revolutions. The ruinous grounds also provided our soccer fields.

As a kid I loved to read Jules Verne, Karl May, and James Fenimore Cooper novels. *Around the World in Eighty Days, Winnetou,* and *The Last of the Mohicans* were my favourites. At age 9 I wrote a story, "The Immortal Cowboy," and let one of my friend's older sister type it for me. It's a definite and unfalsifiable document I kept in my archives, a reminder of my childhood enticement to become a writer. But very soon my interest changed and I wolfed down biographic books about artists, scientists, and revolutionaries. The struggle of heroic revolutionaries captured my imagination and soon directed my interest to utopian anarchist philosophies. Reading about the life stories of famous scientists, I discovered that most of them had strong artistic ambitions before they devoted themselves to science. On the other hand, reading the biographies of great artists, writers, musicians, and revolutionaries, I discovered that many of them studied medicine for a while, though most of them dropped out after a few years. Among them were Apollinaire, Marinetti, Vasarely, André Breton, Brecht, Che Guevara, and many others. I therefore decided that studying medicine was almost obligatory to becoming a great artist, writer, or revolutionary. In my high school years I got bewildered reading Salinger's *The Catcher in the Rye*, Kerouac's *On the Road* and Ginsberg's *Howl*. These three books made my head spin, changed my way of thinking, sharpened my senses, stimulated my imagination … they acted on me as ultimate motivating forces.

I was already a university student when I wrote a critical, satirical, mocking play "The Immortal Writer." In this play, a young and enthusiastic admirer interviews a famous writer who is taking a bath. The admirer wants to learn about the secret of the long and successful career of the writer. But only at the very end of the philosophical drama he finally learns it through the writer's own simple demonstration: while taking a bath he always urinates in the water.

The 1956 Hungarian Revolution was a crucial, decisive, and fascinating experience for my whole life. I saw destruction, blood, fire, desolation from a close distance. I inhaled the damp smell of air raid bunkers. My grandfather made me a toy gun from firewood. I was only seven years old, but I felt like taking part in the fight against the Russians so one day I sneaked out from the air raid shelter to the street, and, from behind a tree, I pointed my toy gun at a Russian tank convoy. A soldier jumped out from the leading armoured vehicle and slowly came towards me at which point I ran back to the building and hid in a dark and cold corner of the basement corridor.

In those days lots of very young kids sacrificed themselves by throwing Molotov cocktails to Russian tanks. I heard the squeaking noise of tanks surrounding our building. For a few hours there was big panic among the residents of the bunker. The Russians were looking for the boy. The janitor, who spoke some Russian, convinced them that everything was in order and there were no revolutionaries inside the building and finally they left. When I came out from hiding the residents of the bunker broke my wooden gun into small pieces in a collective ritual. I like to consider this event my most significant performance piece, one that I have never been able to surpass. To keep the true spirit and creative force of childhood, one must never grow up.

At home I belonged to an intellectual, middle-class family with aristocratic roots in Transylvania from my mother's side. My grandfather was my best friend. He lost nearly all his assets after WWII and was classified by the new communist government as an ex-capitalist exploiter, a potential enemy of the state. I learned to live with double standards. What meant Soviet Liberation in school was called Russian Invasion at home. We celebrated the People of the Great Soviet Union in school and at home we listened to Radio Free Europe's sermon about American Freedom. In school I learned about atheism and at home I took private religious lessons. In school we were taught that collectivism was above all while at home family values ruled our life. Living with double standards was just as clear as confusing and conflicting.

Miraculously my grandfather somehow kept a cottage in Surány, located on an island in the Danube, and that's where our family spent the summers in remote idyllic rural happiness. He and I went on fishing expeditions almost every morning. I was 13 when he suddenly died of cancer, the first tragic loss in my life. I was devastated.

It took me many years to realize that I was completely mind-blinded and brainwashed by the system of education that falsified history and fed us with lies. It was a lesson in deception followed by a rude awakening that planted in me a strong and lasting disillusionment at age 17. I also felt strong disappointment with the conservative views of my family. My father's complete rejection of my creative ambitions was especially humiliating; however, it didn't stop me from doing things. It rather catalyzed my activities. I went through radical changes, gathered self-confidence and extra strength through new artistic experimentation. From then on I committed myself to subverting the system. I turned communist rhetoric into my virtue, and employed it to confront authority and control. Later I implanted it into Neoism. It is now something like a bio-microchip interface under my skin.

⋅ Right after finishing high-school, at the end of May/1967, I took my guitar on a hitchhiking trip from Budapest to Lake Balaton. By then I was completely taken by the idea that I'd become a folk singer, like Bob Dylan, Antoine or Donovan, or someone like the legendary Hungarian poet/singer/historian Sebestyén Lantos Tinódi (1510-1556), and I'd spend my life roaming the country with a shoulder bag and a guitar. So I went for my first experience right away. I even stopped at an underpass to play a song to passers-by but I got stopped by the police and hustled away. And that's how my first hitchhiking plan ended.

Only a year before, at the age of sweet 16, I happened to be in Paris, visiting my father who was there doing some scientific research.

That's when I first closely witnessed a different generation of youth with long hair, wearing jeans, sitting at the bank of the Seine, playing guitar, surrounded by tourists. I wanted to join them and become a street singer too. But I felt embarrassed because my hair was too short and my overall look reflected my father's taste. Right after our arrival with my mom he forced me to have a haircut which for me meant a total disaster. Even though by then I already wrote my own songs and played in a band, Trógerek (Bastards), which I formed with a couple of schoolmates, I lived under the strict control of my father. During the first two nights in Paris I slept alone in a hotel, one floor above of my parents' room, and fantasized about a revolution, fighting for my own freedom, getting rid of my father's dictatorship, taking off, running away, and never returning to the Fatherland. But for that I had to wait ten more years.

My conflicts with my father never ended, and although he was generous in helping me with my daily survival, and at times he even tried to catch on to my activities and grasp my ideas, these were short lived moments. Our antagonistic relationship is immortalized with irony in one of my videos *Revolutionary Song* (2005), based on the above described haircut-confrontation in Paris. It tells about my failed rebellion against him, the embodiment of authoritarian dictator, forcefully taking me to a hairdresser. The satirical script of the video reconnects the 1956 Hungarian Revolution and the May 1968 student revolt in Paris while telling about the clash between father and son.

Regardless the differences between us, I began my studies at the Semmelweis Medical University at age 20. It all started fine; I enjoyed being a student. Before being admitted to medical university, I spent a couple of years working in a hospital and finished a special educational program to became a paramedic nurse. After starting medical university it seemed like finally my father's wishes were going to conclude the future of my life in the Fatherland.

But not everything happened the way he imagined. From then on, I started developing my own personal "system of belief" that has remained a work in progress ever since, under the term of Neoism. It can be defined as a spiritual exercise inspired by confusion, chaos, and mayhem. I took inspiration from all parts of life — misery, history, science, technology, mythology, military terms, porn, robotics, fashion design, alien abduction, conspiracy theories, vampire legends, extraterrestrial cults, religious and political movements, and many other ideas and methods, especially Yoga, Tao, and Wilhelm Reich's orgone energy concept. Catalyzed by Reich's genius, I realized that the accumulation of ideas is a vital life force that can heal people and save the world from total suicide.

Later on all these ideas helped me develop the concept of Neoism. I learned about Reich's work at university and his life and revolutionary ideas fascinated me immediately. Instead of focusing only on anatomy and biochemistry, I also took part in student demonstrations, wrote manifestos in the university paper, and organized happenings in the student club. By doing that, I ran into serious problems first with the political leadership of the university. Soon afterward I was investigated by the secret police for taking part in dissident, subversive activities. I was constantly intimidated and blackmailed by the authorities and as a result I failed my exams. In the end, I had no other choice but to leave university in order to rid myself of police harassment. My family was devastated; my father furious, beside himself.

Dropped out from university and kicked out from home, for the next couple of years I lived like a bum, crashing at friends' places in Budapest or hiding in the country in Surány and elsewhere. For a while I kept performing in clubs, youth-camps, and festivals as a folk singer, either solo or with different bands, under different names, Pop Kantor, Kantor Inform, Drazsé Expressz, until finally I got blacklisted and banned; my songs were considered insurrectionary and my political attitude corrupting the youth. Sometime in 1975, after a forced meeting with a producer at the Hungarian Radio, it was clearer than ever that I had no chances as a singer/songwriter in the Hungarian subculture unless I completely changed into a different person. Soon afterwards, in the Spring 1976, after another meeting, this time with David Zack, an American correspondence artist who happened to have a show at the Young Artists Club in Budapest, it also became clear that there might still be another chance for me to start a new life.

In August, 1976, in the company of my girlfriend Zsuzsa and our two-month-old dog, Bögre (Mug), we fled from Budapest to Paris. By then my sister was already married to a doctor and lived happily with their first daughter in their own downtown Budapest apartment.

My parents were on vacation, so I didn't have to say goodbye to anyone, except to a couple of very trusted friends—a mistake—but luckily we crossed the border. I called my mom when we were already in Switzerland to tell her that I wouldn't return. In Paris I became a subway singer and performed every day at different subway stations, and that's how I made most of my money for daily survival, and got recognition in the local art and music scene. But that's a different story. Shortly before leaving from Budapest we recorded a full album of my songs in a private apartment using a reel-to-reel tape recorder. And that's how my youth ended in Fatherland.

P.S.: *But the struggle between me and my father continued. A constant friction between us remained, establishing an unsolvable conflict that lasted many more long years, basically until his death. While my father worried about me dissipating my energies, wasting my time and squandering my talents, for me "dissipating my energies" was the greatest virtue, "wasting my time" was a redeeming philosophy, and "squandering my talents" was a way of creative living that I planned for my whole life.*

ELDORADO MANIFESTO

1980 feb 14

dear human-beings,

we are the extraterrestrial neoists, temporarily staying on the earth and looking for relationships.

we would like to be your friends and help you to find out a new way of life: the cosmic-urban-eternity.

Tonight we start a long ~~project~~ term project, we call it URBANO FESTO NEOISTO, and we came to the ELDORADO to give you knowledge about it. We declare that from tonight onwards we are responsable for all of the world's events from Japan to Alaska, from the Kremlin to the Moulin Rouge, from the White House to the Eldorado.
We declare that from tonight onwards you are free from political, economic and cultural responsibilities and that the presidents of countries, directors of institutions, traders, parties, Etc. are removed from their positions.
We declare that from tonight onwards money has lost its value.
We declare that from tonight onwards hunger is the mother of beauty.
We declare that from tonight onwards pornography is the national value.
That's enough for now, more to come later.
And thank you for your coming.
Convulsion, subversion, defection.
We are fightfully yours.

The Neoistos

THE MYTH OF SISYPHUS

I'm calling the Devil
and asking him to be the Judge
I'm calling the Devil
and asking him to be the Judge
I keep rolling the Rock
I keep rolling the Rock
I keep rolling the Rock
I keep rolling the Rock
roll the the Rock up the hill
kill your mind shape your will
roll the the Rock up the hill
kill your mind shape your will
the rotten is the fresh
the revolt of the flesh
the rotten is the fresh
the revolt of the flesh
one has to take a stand
be either for or be against

I'm a stranger to myself
I don't know who the hell am I
I'm a stranger to myself
I don't know who the hell am I
I refuse and deny
refuse and deny
deny deny deny
I refuse and deny
roll the the Rock up the hill
kill your mind shape your will
roll the the Rock up the hill
kill your mind shape your will

the rotten is the fresh
the revolt of the flesh
the rotten is the fresh
the revolt of the flesh
one has to take a stand
be either for or be against

THE ART OF REBELLION

*"The only way to deal with an unfree world is to become so
absolutely free that your very existence is an act of rebellion."*
—**Monty Cantsin** (Albert Camus)

I SIGNED THIS ALBERT CAMUS quote as Monty Cantsin sometime in
the 80s, and adapted it as a plunder statement that perfectly fits into
the Book of Neoism. I also appropriated it as a template for making
other statements such as the following one:

> The only way to deal with art in a totalitarian world is to
> become absolutely free from institutional control and museum
> dictatorship that your very existence is an art of rebellion.
> But how can someone implement such an idea into a creative
> practice in today's extremely control-freak authoritarian society?
> What chances anyone can have to succeed in the realization of
> Monty Cantsin Albert Camus's magisterial pronouncement?

I'm a refugee. An art criminal. I come from nowhere and I belong
nowhere. It's always 6 o'clock. Past=Present=Future. I have never been
interested in postmodern formulas of making art. I rather wasted my
time as an eternal outsider refusing the norms of society for the sake
of my own socio-political engagement. I often wonder what kept me
from selling my soul to the authoritarian system. Why didn't I sign a
production deal with the divine driving forces of the art world just like
a popstar would do with music managements and record companies?
The idea of creating overproduced largescale installations for museums
that were built to represent the power of spectacle always repulsed
me. I am frightened by the possibility that one day my work will be
discredited by the sponsorship of the murderous corporate mainstream
culture's leading financial institutions such as the Rentagon and the
Bank of Broadcast Imperialism.

During the night,
when the curtain is down in Totalitaria,
I can hear the rumbling noise of tanks moving through

the stage of my everyday life, and,
during the day, when the curtain is up,
I see the bulldozers crushing the buildings:
Gentrification – Eviction – Extermination – Genocide.
The Spectacle of Noise,
Misery, Greed and Stupidity.

But I never wanted to be a lonely landscape painter either. As a matter of fact I never wanted to be an artist. I wanted to become a revolutionary. But instead of heading straight to the barricades waving a red flag in one hand and holding a flaming steam iron in the other, I took a course at a paramedic nurse school and then went to medical university. At the same time I also wrote poetry, practiced art and took part in activist movements. Art, science, revolution … My plan "A" was to follow the path of Che Guevara. In case of losing the game, my plan "B" was to disappear somewhere far, perhaps in Asia or Africa, like my other hero Arthur Rimbaud did.

Growing up in a communist country in Eastern Europe determined my future life events. I got educated in a world of dictatorships, insurrections, double standards, personality cult, brainwashing propaganda, chaos, convulsion, blood, fire, destruction, ruins … I was surrounded by the ghosts of revolutionary movements, zombies of social insurrections, demons of future rebellions. It was a fascinating experience, just as hopeless as full of desires and expectations. Very decadent. My aesthetics was shaped by both, a totalitarian system and a conservative family with aristocratic roots in Transylvania.

I was already in my early 20s when I finally followed my own instincts, and, like a sleepwalker or rather sleepswimmer I crossed the Seven Seas. From that moment everything happened really fast just like a blitzkrieg. I took over the late 70s and then invaded the 80s. There was a free spirited communication network, known as mail-art, that helped me to get in touch with other refugee types in all parts of the globe. I sent out information about the Neoist Conspiracy and proposed to everyone to become part of it. *"Call yourself Monty Cantsin and do everything in the name of Neoism"*, was the magic sentence and the only rule. Everything else was up to the users of the names.

In today's technological sense Neoism can be interpreted as an early social interface. I called the network World Wide Neoist Web. This was around 1980, fifteen years before the official WWW and the invasion of cyberspace. I became the false prophet of Neoism in the East Side of Montreal, across the street from the Blood Factory, and later on I moved closer to the riots in New York's Lower East Side. It was a rebellious decade when changes took place all over the world. Punk and new wave music wiped out the authority of rock'n'roll. A new haircut philosophy transformed the look of youth. A redeeming chaos and anarchy took over the streets. The flower children of the hippie peace movement were killed by a sudden stroke. Free haircuts were the best propaganda action for Neoism.

I initiated the Neoist Apartment Festival concept in 1979, in Montreal, by opening my own apartment as a centre for performance events and other subvertainment. That was the only way to free ourselves from the oppressive system of galleries, museums and other institutions. We had no interest and time to send them exhibition proposals to produce shows two or three years later. We didn't exactly know what we wanted but we wanted it immediately. And our proposals were always rejected anyway. Therefore we gave up working with them and started our own illegal organizations.

We gave the finger to the unfree world of Cold War led by the Soviets and the USA. We declared our independence from the art system and turned our existence into a sci-fi novel, populated by illegal aliens, extraterrestrials, cults, conspirators, vampires, demons, shapeshifters, porn stars, superheroes ... In many ways we have realized what Camus originally said in the above quote.

I was always much more interested in the activation of dead spaces than producing art objects in my studio for museum shows. Invading abandoned buildings and ruined military bunkers were among my favourite activities. Making work directly in museums, in the form of illegal surprise interventions, was much more exciting than daydreaming in my studio. My best known method is the splashing of my own blood on museum walls.

This dynamic gesture, critically labelled as vandalism, instantly triggers reaction and activates the whole machinery of the art system. It alarms the security, confronts the museum directors, summons the police, appeals to the legal system, invites the media, excites the consumers of information … It usually grows into an all encompassing durational and basically never ending work in progress. In 1979 when I began the Blood Campaign project my goal was to finance the operations of Neoism by selling my blood as an art object. I predicted that by 1984 my blood would reach the value of one million dollars per milliliter. In order to increase the value of my blood, I created scandals, conflicts, confrontations, critical situations. My museum interventions were n essential part of the value making process. I got arrested, jailed, banned. Soon my mugshots were pinned up on the walls above the security desks in art museums.

In 1988 I was charged with $10-million in damages for defacing one of Picasso's most important masterpieces, "Girl with Mirror", with a few drops of my blood, in the Museum of Modern Art, New York. I took this charge as an official recognition of my work and an acknowledgment of the value of my blood as a work of art. While locked up in a detention facility in New York, squashed in a tiny prison cell with about a dozen high profile criminals, I figured out the equation of the Art of Rebellion. It's written in blood, imprinted in my brain, engraved in my heart and tattooed in my soul:

Blood=Life=Existence=Rebellion=Art

PERFORMANCE IN THE 80S

The 80s never have been the 80s
and never will be the 80s
the 80s started in the 70s
and it's still not over yet
the 80s started in the 50s
or rather in the 30s or even before
and the 80s was the 60s and 70s
and there was no 80s ever
the 80s remained in the shadow of the 80s
and the shadow of the 80s was the 80s
and the 80s was shadowed by itself
and none could see the 80s
hear the 80s no one touched the 80s

I fucked the 80s
I got fucked by the 80s
and got fucked up by the 80s
fucked over by the 80s
I know everything about the 80s
because I was right there and I was there
all the way through the 80s
and before the 80s and after the 80s
covered by the transparent body of the 80s
by the transparent hole of the bloody abyss
of the void of the nothing
I filled the full length of the emptiness
I invaded the depth the 80s
I was the spectre of the 80s
hired by 14 Secret Masters of the World
I only knew that I was there
without being there
in the shadow of the 80s

none of my friends lived in the 80s
they left the 80s before the 80s began
they moved back to the 60s and became
terrorists, they moved ahead into the 90s
and became scientists
everybody was
singing like a lunatic alien great
great grandmother-machine
one thousand light years
away from her origin dying
in a golden age home in Kananga
pa-pa-pa-pa pa-pa-pa-pa pa-pa-pa-pa
pa pa pa pa pa pa pa pa pa-pa-pa-pa
that is so boring that you laugh and laugh
and laugh until you get sick and vomit
and vomit and vomit until
you feel better and start your life again
by committing suicide just for fun because
it's a great experience to commit suicide
and everybody has to try it to know what it is

and that's what we learned in the 80s
of suicide or the suicide of the 80s
we were so many trying to learn suicide
suicide for self-defence
behind the spotlights we were beyond the
the spotlights that were not spotlights
the spotlights were just black holes
in the universal destruction of birthday cakes
and there were too many
oily plaster monger landlord
vampires to whisper to in despair

oh yes the 80s was gone before it could begin
and it never even happened
and I don't really want to start it again
I don't even want to talk about it

and look like a stupid idiot
shadowed by the dead bodies of the stars
and the anti-stars who were me and them
and them were them and I was I
and we were all baked with the spirit
of chocolate philosophies that were so
tasteless that everyone could enjoy it
without any problem with the police
and the army and the government

I cried to my Mother
and Father and Sister and Grandmother
and a whole group of the sparkling urine
shit pus blood of the fucked up universe in
Montreal that was composed from
cultural fuck offs
who were deported back from the 90s and
were kicked out from the 70s
all these heroic criminals and
fuckyou comrades and blood sisters
standing in line in the Lower East Side
at the food banks and soup kitchens
writing the story of total suicide
and composing a love song for Madonna's cunt
that she is still hiding in her vagina
way up stuck to the wall of her rectum eyes
of the 80s blindfolded
gazing into the black mirror
of my life story while

the hot bowls of misery were
boiling in the backroom of the street riots
that never took place
the cheeeezy story of revolution
that never took place
only the films were produced and reproduced
and I was forced to self-destroy with a

black dildo right in the head and the eyes and the nose
and the ears and the bellybutton against the ideals
of communism and international fuck off confusion
the 80s was way toooooo long and boring war that
no one should try it again because there was nothing in the 80s that you
couldn't find in the 90s and couldn't find in the 70s or in the 1940s
I immigrated to the 80s exiled to the 80s I was deported by the 80s
evicted into the 80s and destroyed by the 80s and resurrected in the
80s my blood was the only value of the 80s the only exchange for sex
the only gold for the flag
the only shit for the landlords
the only drink for the executioners taking a hot bath during X-mas
time and laughing at the moon that was me
my face my ass my balls my heart

the 80s were all about me and only me
nobody else was there to see my misery growing in the Lower East Side
and in the Lowereastsides of the entire universe
and all over the place on the bus on my way
from Chicoutimi to San Francisco I sucked
plastic bombs and licked supersonic machine-cunts
until the machines ripped out my tongue and
my bloody tongue ripped out
my lung and stomach and veins
and I exposed them all at the Final Stop Museum that was only there
temporarily for a couple of hours so we could drink a tea in the
cafeteria and listen to Buddha's instructions on the tv-headphones

the 80s never have been the 80s
and never will be the 80s
the 80s started in the 70s
and it's still not over yet
the 80s started in the 50s
or rather in the 30s or even before
and the 80s was the 60s and 70s
and there was no 80s ever

I was there in the shadows of the
gentrified neighbourhoods of the 80s
holding up a flaming steam iron and singing
the bleeding anthem of Neoism
tratatatatatatata
I was invisible so much that I couldn't even see my own
cunt in the black mirror masturbating
in front of the unknown members of the firing squad
of the post-trans-anti-para-tech-ultra-whatever
society of the speculators
tratatatatatatata
Amen!

*In 1998 I was commissioned by Le Lieu in Québec city to create a
performance dedicated to the 80s for their ART ACTION 1958-1998
event. I wrote this rhapsodic text to be recited during my performance.*

NEOISM NEOISM NOISM NEOISM NEOISM NEOISM NEOISM NEOISM NEOISM NEOISM NEOISM NEOISM NEOISM NEOISM NEOISM NEOISM
ISM NEOSIM NEOISM NEOISM NEOISM NEOISM NEOISM NEOISM NEOISM NEOISM NEOISM NEOISM NEOISM NEOISM NEOISM JE
M NEOISM NEOISM NEOISM NEOISM NEOISM NEOISM NEOISM NEOISM NEOISM NEOISM NEOISM NEOISM

Communiqué
News Release

ENTER INTO ETERNITY
COZMIK-URBAN-ETERNITY
ETERNAL IMMORTALITY
TOTAL RFEEDOM OF HUMAN BRAIN
TOTAL FREEDOM OF HUMAN DREAM
TOTAL FREEDOM OF HUMAN LOVE
TOTAL FREEDOM OF HUMAN WILL

NO WORK
NO ART
NO MONEY

convulsion
subversion
defection

NEOISM 'We have all we need to make the people's life even better'

monty cantsin'

extraterrestial business man, spy and Neoist.

TOTAL SUICIDE OR ETERNAL IMMORTALITY

NEOISM is nothing more than all that we do in the name of NEOISM

we are the neoists and we are looking for
relationships, we would like to be your friends and help you
discover a new way of life: cosmic-urban-eternity.
we have started a long-term project we call it the 'URBANO-
FESTO-NEOISTO and have come here to contribute of saying the earth
at this time we do not see any possibility of this in our best for ster-
from total suicide. however, in spite of this and to do our best for ster-
to change the condition of the world and to do our best for the future.
our conspiracy is the potential energy energy of the future.
we are not subject to the lies of science,
we are rightfully yours.
that's enough for now, more to come later.
and in the name of all neoists we declare that we love you

thank you for your attention

M. KANTZIN

MAY 14/80, EARTH,

MY GALLERY TOUR

June 15th, 2006.

Hydro is supposed to shut down my electricity today because I didn't pay my bills for a few months. I owe them something like a lousy $330. Fuck. And the Rentagon is after me for not paying rent for about three months now. My bank accounts are already suspended. But the light is still on and so is my computer. I got some time to write before darkness comes.

***

Presently I have a show at Engine Gallery. A tribute to 1956. Only few people know about the Hungarian Revolution here. But for me it's a question of life and death. Everything that happened to me in my life is the result of 1956. I was 6 years old. I absorbed everything. I got inspired for life. Desolation. Blood. Fire. The rhythmic beat of machineguns. Death. Bombed out buildings and gardens. Burned out tanks. The beauty of failure. I mean failed revolutions.

***

This is basically my first commercial gallery exhibition. Fifty-six new mixed media pieces on wood and canvas. Something I like doing but rarely exhibit. I have thousands of drawings, paintings, objects, mixed media, and sculptural works in my archives. Although we decided to put up three fake red dots to inspire potential buyers, we didn't sell anything yet. It's a total failure. I'm in a total financial disaster. I've been living in the bunker for several months now. But there is always hope.

***

Sandy is telling me for weeks now that I should talk to Nicholas Metivier. He has a gallery on King Street, at Spadina. I never had luck with commercial galleries. I basically only exhibited in my own studio spaces, in artist-run centres, and other non-profit places. This morning I went to Sandy's place after riding my daughter Nineveh (10) to school. Babylon (13), my second son, didn't want to go to school today. And Jericho (15) didn't show up last night. Probably he had a sleepover at his friend Chester's.

***

Today I finally rode my bike to the Metivier Gallery. Before that I had coffee with Sandy and Ildiko at the Drake. Ildiko is a Hungarian originally from Transylvania. Sandy is my girlfriend from Toronto via Calgary. She is a violinist at the Canadian Opera Company. It was her idea that I should meet Metivier.

***

There is an article in *NOW* magazine about my show, written by Kevin Temple, with a colour picture of "The Queen of Neoism," a neoist propaganda portrait version of the ex-Governor General of Canada. I got inspired by her when we met in Ottawa. Since then she is my icon. She is part of the revolutionary mythology of Neoism.

***

Sandy left for rehearsal and I went to Engine Gallery to see if there was anything new. Nothing. We put up Kevin's article on the wall. Before she left, Sandy made me promise that I'll talk to Metivier today. "I believe he is the man to represent your work."

***

My first try to get represented by a commercial gallery in Toronto was in the early 90s. I called up Olga Korper. She said she would never come to my studio. Not even if she would like my work. "There are about 215 artists on the list before you," she said. Then I talked to Chris Cutts. He came to visit a couple of times and we started planning a show, but suddenly he backed out. He said his other gallery artists would leave him if he would take me in.

***

Meanwhile some of the curators from the Power Plant came for visits. Louise Donpierre said she would consider a show if I had shown my work in a gallery before. She seemed to like one of my kinetic file cabinets. But soon afterwards she left the Power Plant. Then came Richard Rhodes. He got excited about my file cabinet sculptures. Sorry, maybe Richard came before Louise, I'm confused now. Lots of changes were happening. The next was Philip Monk. He spent a day sitting in silence in my studio on Richmond Street West. A few weeks later he finally told me on the phone that he hated my work. He called me an outdated, old-fashioned revolutionary, someone who doesn't fit into the post-modern gallery system. He was damn right.

***

So I stopped calling institutions and commercial galleries. I still tried places like Mercer Union and YYZ. The non-profiters. Up until the late 90s I only got rejection after rejection. In 1999, I finally got a solo show of my robotic file cabinet installation at InterAccess. The building was shaking but everyone got used to it. When the show was over, people were telling me that they missed the noise. When the revolution was over, we came out of the bunker and everything was silent. We walked among dead bodies and blown-up military vehicles on the streetcar tracks.

***

I basically never wanted to have gallery shows. I wanted to leave the gallery system. As far as possible. Museums = Prisons. "Get away from the prison of art, build open-situations that permit anyone to act, react, destroy, create." This quote is from an early Neoist pamphlet "Love Letter," which I wrote in 1979, in Montreal. Montreal seemed to have more hunger for this kind of stuff. I had shows in almost every artist-run centre, club, and bar throughout the 80s. I even got featured at the Musée d'art contemporain in 1985. But then came the takeover of the yuppies in the late 80s and Neoism seemed to be over.

***

I relocated to New York. Actually I shared my time between New York and Montreal from 1982. But I only moved there in the summer of 1986. Almost instantly I became spokesman for the Rivington School, New York's radical artist-criminals. I declared myself Self-Appointed Leader of the People of the Lower East Side. I mostly exhibited at underground venues like No Se No, Gas Station, and at the Rivington Sculpture Garden. But I also had shows at the Stockwell Gallery, Franklin Furnace, Kitchen, Generator, Gallery 128, and in all the clubs from the Limelight to the Tunnel via Pyramid, Chameleon, Area, The World …

***

Gentrification hit the Lower East Side hard by the end of the 80s. The Tompkins Square Riot was the last holdout of the homeless and the poor. It involved the whole artist community including the Rivington School. I was planning a revolution with Peter Missing (of Missing Foundation) years before. It finally happened in 1988. There were tanks and helicopters. The cops of course beat the shit out of everyone. I extended the fight against police brutality to the MOMA with a fresh blood-X between two Picassos. The MOMA first declared $10 million in damages. The prosecutor 2nd degree felony. Up to ten years in the ass. Two years of trials later I was given a sentence of 6 months or $1000 fine. Who wants to be in prison? The Foufoune in Montreal organized for me a fundraiser concert / performance.

***

All these things come to my mind as I'm trying to write down some of my experiences with galleries. Especially commercial galleries. After I received the Governor General's Award in 2004, I got interest from

Fabrice at Artcore. He actually exhibited Joseph Beuys around that time, which boosted my confidence in talking to him. I was dead broke that time as well. He tried to sell my works at art fairs, but nothing happened. At least I made him buy a Governor General pancarte from me for $1000. It's probably still in his office. But 6 months later I broke our verbally-made exclusivity contract. Again: who wants to be in prison?

***

I have been in jails and in prisons about a dozen times. I definitely had more "exhibitions" in prisons than in museums. In New York the cops asked me to make a "blood-X" on the jail cell with the ink they use for fingerprints. "You are going to be famous," they said. In Ottawa they tricked me and made me sign a release form in the darkness of the cell. "You are free," the guard said in the middle of the night. I'm not sure if I was ever free. In Budapest, in 1997, almost 10 years after the so-called political changes, I got arrested at the opening of my exhibition at the Black Black Gallery. "You fucking communist, faggot, stinky jew," one of the arresting officers yelled at me as they were clubbing my head while trying to push me into a police car. In front of a TV camera and hundreds of onlookers. In my cell I scratched a poem on the wall. I'm sure they cleaned it up. The video tape also mysteriously disappeared.

***

I've been tempted to commit suicide for about a few months now. I seriously consider this possibility almost every day. When you have a family of three kids and you can't buy them enough food and clothing, it makes you feel like shit. And when the banks start calling you everyday because you are late in your payments, you become more and more desperate. Meanwhile the landlord kicks the door almost every morning for the cheques. I already gave up my cell phone; my cable TV was disconnected a long time ago; and I asked Enbridge to cut off the gas. My studio used to be heated with gas. When Chris and Steve proposed that I have a show at Engine, I was totally desperate. I accepted it right away. And I expected to sell works.

***

When Kevin came to interview me for *NOW*, he asked me if this was the end of my revolution because now I'm showing in a commercial gallery. "Kevin, I have to finance not only my family but the revolution as well." I don't have an academic teaching job like many of my artist friends do, neither do I have any other job. I'm a full time Neoist, whatever that means.

***

I didn't receive a grant for a long time. For 5 years from the Canada Council and 8 years from Ontario. The $15,000 Governor General's Award in 2004 was gone to debts immediately. It wasn't enough to pay my debts and everyone wanted their money immediately. So I had to borrow again. And when debts accumulate misery accumulates. Bills accumulate. Problems accumulate. Will a gallery solve your problems? There is always hope even in a desperate tango. But how long can you do this when you are completely deprived from funding? At the Great Hall meeting of the Canada Council about a year ago, I produced a begging performance in the street, holding the Governor General's picture in one hand. And it wasn't just a "performance," I meant it.

***

When the AGO finally expressed interest in my work and a couple of the curators came to visit my studio, I expected changes. After several visits they said they wanted to purchase my archives, some of my installations, and my blood in the walls project. This was just a couple of months ago, or less. I asked them for immediate help. I mean I asked for an advance to be able to put my archives in order, select the works, and design the blood action. "We can't pay your rent," was the answer. "Think of this as your retirement." I don't think I'll ever retire, but it looks like this deal will never happen anyway. No calls anymore, no visits or talks. $350 million for a façade. Fuck the artist's life.

***

It is much more difficult to be excluded from a museum than to be included. It's even more difficult to be banned from a museum when you are an artist. How many other artists are banned from museums besides me? I know that there are many thousands of artists whose works are included. What's so great in that? I only have one work in one museum: in the National Gallery of Canada. But I'm banned from the National Gallery of Canada. Hahaha.

***

A few months ago I returned to the National Gallery to protest my ban. I was stopped at the main entrance to the building. I could still hand them my affidavit I registered at the Supreme Court of Ontario. I'm taking the National Gallery to court. The hearing is coming up in July 2006. Another reason not to commit suicide right now. Though my main reasons are my kids and my girlfriend. Besides I'll never commit suicide. My death will be a revolutionary act whatever it will be.

***

Actually Philip, who was so against my work in the mid 90s, gave me several shows at several institutions in the 00s. A group exhibition at the Power Plant and a solo show at the Art Gallery of York University. The AGYU show was beautiful. Finally something I really enjoyed creating for an art gallery. But I was dead broke throughout the preparation and during the show. I didn't receive any assistance from anywhere. The Gallery paid me $2500 for a work that took me a year to develop and several weeks to install. My rent is $1600 a month. Why should I commit suicide when this city is killing me anyway?

***

Yes, finally I went to the Nicholas Metivier Gallery. On my bike from Engine Gallery. The receptionist was a beautiful, blond, cold, trendy woman. "Mr. Metivier only receives people by appointment." "I know," I said, "but my girlfriend Sandy suggested me that I just walk in and talk to him. She had a dream about this." Her face stayed expressionless. "You can leave a message." She handed me a piece of paper and a pen. "Hi Nicholas, Sandy, my girlfriend had a dream that you were the right person to represent my work. Many regards, Istvan."

Self-portrait, 1981

LITANY

I'M CONSTANTLY RECREATING MYSELF. My mind is a mutating bio-machine.

Every second is a new definition and there is no best and no linear progression. I'm defined by contradictions, impossible ideas, utopian theories, speculations, stolen information, puns, metathesis, confusion, chaos, terror, paranoia, sex, hedonic gratification, self-destructive misery, weirdness, danger, obscure symbolism, and every manner of direction. The important areas of experimentation are those which produce errors in compensation and provoke an emergency in response. I am the construction of a new convulsive robot-platform philosophy based on the power of electricity. I make a quantum jump every so often and land myself in a new reality-matrix. Intelligence must increase as consciousness expands, or we get burned-out.

I am so deplorably elastic that I can only be a negative idea to the uninitiated, and I can create growing ambiguities which can be annoying to say the least. I use intensity/confusion as weapons to actually force a choice. I have an extreme degree of intensity to break existing aesthetic categories and reject all forms and products.

But what appears today be either a noise-wall or a non-interpretable foreign signal, will tomorrow be considered simplistically familiar.

Critics say that I am a single-minded, one-dimensional fanatic dedicated to figuring out actions that would irritate people and make their life unbearable. Conflicts bring out the best in me because I am used to confrontation. I feel great in critical situations when I have to make very fast decisions and get myself out of trouble. My job is to show up at public places and tell people to burn down their own houses if they want to be happy. I am an extreme metaphor for an extreme situation. My mind is a kit of desperate measures only for use in an extreme crisis. My mind is the place where everything happens, where everything involves me. I am a fanatic lover of myself, considering me as the only condition under which I can exist, develop and grow.

I was floating through the sky on a warm sunny evening. I gradually came to rest on a grassy cliff top. I could spend hours there reading or daydreaming, enjoying solitude until night fell. It was all beautiful and idyllic. The birds were singing and there was a smell of wild flowers. By dint of pondering different thoughts my intelligence grew sharper and my ideas gained precision. But suddenly I felt I was rotten through and through and hung like a decaying carcass, losing my limbs, oozing pus, and I could barely keep, in the general corruption of my body, a few words in my mouth. Under the lowering sky, in the humid atmosphere, the horror of life became more apparent and the grip of spleen more oppressive; a craving for pleasures took hold of me.

Right now I'm lying in bed, touching my body all over, wetting and kissing myself. I'm rubbing and feeling my body. There are bright lights and mirrors all around so I can fully admire myself. I wish to explore inner space, that psychological domain where the inner world of the mind and the outer world of reality meet and fuse. I work my hair up into heaps of curls, all tied with tiny, pale-blue ribbons. I admire my breasts in the mirror. I hold each one in my hands and feel its firmness and tickle the nipples so they get hard and they grow.

The complete elimination of oppression is a difficult task in a world which bears the marks of many thousand years of government propaganda. There are huge abysses between my intentions and achievements. I am rapaciously conditioned all the time, I often find myself trapped in ideological stances which I know to be bizarre, but I can't struggle out from under. My phobia of role-entrapment compels me to ridicule the values of society. I just don't enjoy the pleasures other people enjoy. My cock is in my right hand now. I love to suck it and lick my cunt at the same time. The fact is that I am more than me, so as a consequence of this fact I'll never become completely what I already am. My life takes up its position as a dataclysmic philosophy of today. I am the obvious counter-strategy that emerges spontaneously. I am full of illogical things and events that people may never understand. I'm waiting for a phone call which, if it ever comes, comes because it's a wrong number.

As a young boy I saw my family as a prison. My teachers told me how to think and what to be. They instilled in me a deep expectation of living for the future. They never told me that tomorrow never comes and when tomorrow comes, it is today. I looked at my dear father and sweet mother and vowed not to repeat their lives. I escaped from the Fatherland, broke free from the Motherland. I'm not a fixed, self-enclosed social system but rather a definite trend in the historic development of alien-kind, which, in contrast with the intellectual guardianship of all clerical and governmental institutions, strives for the free unhindered unfolding of all the individual forces in life. Like paper I endure anything. I recognize no restrictions other than those determined by the lies of my own subindividual transnature, which cannot properly be regarded as restrictions since these lies are not imposed by any outside legislator beside or above me, but are immanent and inherent, forming the very basis of my own material.

I am the uprising of a moment that springs up and out of time and violates the lies of science. I am the forbidden moment, an unforgivable denial of the dialectic, shimmying up the pole and out of the obscure and wet smokehole. I take my own abstractions for realities. I am almost self-explanatory. I should be understood without difficulty, understood in action. If my life doesn't make any kind of sense at all than don't impose a meaning on me. It's better to remain in doubt than to try to make something mean what it may not really mean at all. I'm freed of time and place, but spatiotemporally chained to the noise of the events. My consciousness is chemical in nature and changes as its chemistry changes.

To elaborate on this more than confusing statement I would have to analyze the contradictory character of my anti-philosophical speculation. But this is impossible, or, perhaps somebody else should do it. I can't. What I'm interested in is to accumulate seemingly useless information in a form that is satisfactory to initiate chemical impulses in my brain. Well, I'm not even sure about that. But why should I be preoccupied with the goal of my ideas? Can the answer be a simply chemical procedure? A diffuse rationalism, the levelling impress of the mass media, the increasing monochrome of the technological milieu, are crowding on the private components of marvel and fantasy.

Under the stress of the media, even our dreams are standardized and made synchronic with those of our neighbours. With someone that you know really well you can transmit information brain to brain, get the concepts across so fast that you get to the point where it's hard to tell who's who. It would be possible to link together a large number of brains through multi-sensory communication and create a brain-net or brain-forest. In fact that's what all the communication networks are about. But this communication should be done without indirect brain extending devices, tools such as the computer or pen and paper, using direct transmission only.

Since the average North American is bombarded by 300 ad jingles and soundbites per day, they develop what we call "the communication phallus". It takes a powerful word or phrase to stimulate the phallus.

The superficial perversity of my hermaphroditism is at heart an unresolved conflict between reverence and ridicule. Condemned to shallowness, it is compelled to recast its most trivial experiences as existential monodramas. I want to write a series of fucked-up philosophical-essays about the present confusion of thinking, individual isolation, alienation, introspection and techno-sophistication. The marriage of reason and nightmare which has dominated the 20th century has given birth to an ever more ambiguous game. We live in a world ruled by fictions of every kind—political propaganda, pop-culture mythology, mass media imagery, etc. We live inside an enormous novel. It is less and less necessary to invent a fiction since it has been already written.

jan 28,1989 Montreal

H.R.Fricker
CH-9043 Trogen
Switzerland

AMBASADA NEOIST
1020 Lajoie ave.
H2V 1N4 Canada   tel. 514-273-2801

you powerful white man,
remember the buffalo and the Iroquois!,remember the Sioux and
the German Jews, remember the black slaves..there are too many
things to remember!? you are part of the death apparatus, you
belong to the Network of Killing, your government is a genocidal
machine... this is a war of survival, there is no time to talk
about peace and love, there is no time for orgies, nobody has the
power to paint giant genitals on the walls of airports, train
stations ,yes, I'm talking about the holy network of humanity,
and I'm confused,The Great Confusion: the essence of Neoism,
          I address this letter to all of you: mail-artists,
          shitheads, assholes, tourists,networkers,neoists,and
all the   oppressors of the world, the weapons
of death   have been perfected, no marksmen are
needed any   more, the means of self-destruction
are within   every one of us, and you know that,
we live this   way, new networks of depression are
naturally   organized by the fear of society,
I cant talk   about art anymore, what are arts and
literatures   if their grandest productions are hordes
of   faith   ful slaves?, I DENY ALL THINGS!, that's how

                   creation begins, we were born into perpetual
                       conflicts, that's what we call
                   CONDITION OF COMBAT,Neoism is
simply a   result of this ready-made)situation,
it's   also a solution for a x new way
of living   cosmik-urban-eternity(1979),
EVERY   ARTISTS PAINT WITH BLOOD, that's
how we   make gold or GOLD, the victor
gets   the gold and the land every time,
TOWARDS AKADEMGO   ROD, the promised land of Neoism,
this is our road, we'll win, why should the delights
of life go to   cowards?, our conspira cy is the
potencial energy   of the future, the International
Neoist Network   represent a powerful and laughing
lust-machinary of total collective positive plagiarism,
the most subtle   menace to the survival of
authoritarianism, Akademgorod all mechanisms of logic
are broken, control is impossible, here we are, this is
a love letter, this is not a love letter, just a text about
neoism and network- art, I'm here and you are there, and
between us the and oceans:reality, all I want is to
suck tits   eat pussy and feel like the child who
catches a   glimpse of the lighted Christmas tree
through a   crack in the closed door, Neoism
has been   developed trhough bed-room lectures,
correspondence, here is the message of the 14 Secret Masters of
the Universe:the bell tells because someone is pulling the rope,
join neoism and never die, feel the world's breath against your skin,

                              seize the day! seize the night!

End== Monty Cantsin
ps.television never sleeps!   your immortal friend
                                       monty cantsin   Istvn

THE REBEL SLAVE

A slave who has taken orders all his life
Suddenly decides he cannot obey anymore
This has been going on too long
This has been going on too long
Another slave, who has taken orders all her life,
Suddenly decides that she cannot obey anymore.
This has been going on too long
This has been going on too long
And then all the slaves, everywhere,
Suddenly decide that they cannot obey anymore.
This has been going on too long
This has been going on too long
From the moment the rebel slaves find their voices
– Even though they say nothing but "no" –
They begin to desire and to judge
This has been going on too long
This has been going on too long
Besides rejecting the conditions of slavery
And refusing to obey the humiliating orders,
The slaves proclaim their own demands
Now or Never!
Now or Never!
Now or Never!
Now or Never!
This has been going on too long
This has been going on too long
Awareness, no matter how confused it may be,
Develops from every act of rebellion.
The slaves suddenly adopt an attitude of
All or Nothing!
All or Nothing!
All or Nothing!
All or Nothing!

This has been going on too long
This has been going on too long
This has been going on too long
This has been going on too long

THE GREAT CONFUSION
a revolution / a solution / an open situation /a game

CALL YOURSELF

MONTY CANTSIN

DO EVERYTHING IN THE NAME OF

NEOISM

a message from **MONTY CANTSIN**
self appointed leader of the people of
The Lower East Side,
*open -pop-star, immortal
revolutionary and hard-art singer*

UNDISCLOSED LOCATION

It takes place in an old, dark, abandoned, prison like place, furnished with simple benches, chairs, a table ...

1/ A number of people are in the room, most of them are somewhat sick, coughing, vomiting, angry ...

Steve: Hi everyone. I am Steve. I am your host. Do you know why are you here?

One: No! We don't know! We have no idea what the fuck is happening. And we want to be freed immediately! (he spits, he is really sick, sweating ...)

Two: Our freedom is being violated right now!

Steve: Yes, of course. I understand. You think that your personal freedom has been violated and you were brought here against your will ... That's right. You can't even move, you are sick, tied up, you are prisoners. But you agreed to be part of this mission, otherwise you wouldn't be here. We tied you up for your own protection.

Two: Motherfuckers!

Three: What's going on in here? Are we part of some experiment of madness? Some kind of an absurd game?

Steve: Hot! You are hitting the nail! That's exact. You are here to be part of something like a collective experiment, a historical event ...

One: I knew that some insane idiot has done this. Some bloody retard who wants to take over the world and kill everyone ...

Maestro: It's me that insane idiot.

Two: What, you? You kidnapped us and locked us in this shithole? How the fuck we got here?!

Steve: Ladies and gentlemen, let me introduce you to the mastermind of this happening, the Maestro.

Maestro: Yes, it was my idea to bring you here.

Three: Where the hell are we? And how did we get here?

Maestro: It's a very special and specific location. It has a nature that can be only described as supernatural. It's like abstract art in opposing the reality of landscape.

Four: It seems to me that I'm in the reality of a lunatic asylum under the control of some abstract maniacs.

Steve: Skepticism won't help us. You have to accept our scenario or we will fail.

Four: What scenario?!

Maestro: Perhaps it's time to explain a few things before we start the transmission.

One: Transmission? Give me back my cell phone so I can call for help.

Maestro: We don't need any devices here. This building is itself a transmission unit. As I told you this location has a very specific nature. It's almost like a black hole, a zero-zone that is charged with so much extra power that it's impossible to locate. It can function as a broadcasting unit that converts telepathic waves into audiovisual signals and overlay them on any frequencies of data.

Four: Have you seen a shrink lately?

Maestro: Well, yes, actually I'm a psychiatrist and I also brought one of my colleagues with me.

Psychiatrist: Hi everyone, I'm Elisabeth. I do research in death, the greatest mystery in science. I'm also working in the fields of psychotronic science, brain to brain direct communication better known as telepathic transmission. The Maestro hired me to be his adviser.

One: A bunch of mad scientists! Oh Lord! I'm very tired, I'm sick, my body hurts, I can't listen to this nonsense!

Steve: We are going to free you, give you some medication, and serve you some food and drinks in a minute.

Maestro: Escape plans are useless. This location basically doesn't exist. And by the way ... we are here to start a revolution!

2/ They are finishing dinner around a table ... It is packed with food and drinks. The ambience has changed and everyone seems to be fine and relaxed.

Four: Okay Maestro, that was awesome! I don't even ask how you catered this heavenly supper ... you can keep your secret ... but are you going to tell us about the plan?

One: How do you want to start a revolution … from here? From this location of nowhere? With us?

Two: Where is the rebel army?

Three: Where are the weapons?

Maestro: We don't need anything but you! Everything will be done through your minds, using the oldest method of transmission … telepathy!

One: In other words through brainwashing.

Maestro: Right! But in the good sense of the term! We are determined to open up the channels rather than tighten security measures … The chains of submissiveness have to be broken! We have to liberate the masses from under the mind-blinding control of broadcast media corporations, the banks, the Rentagon, the Politburo and all the oppressive forces of governmental authorities …!!!

Psychiatrist: Maestro! Slow down please! I know you are excited to start the process but we have to tell them some other details first … you know

Steve: Yes, she is right, Maestro. They have to know about all the risks and sacrifice.

One: So there will be some blood?

Three: Do we have to die for the revolution?

Maestro: I'm a bit surprised to hear this … Don't you realize, my dear, that you are already dead!?

Four: Seeing Marilyn and Andy among us I kind of suspected that some of us were probably ghosts … but I didn't know I was also on the list of deceased.

Four: How did you brought us back?

Psychiatrist: That was the least problematic part of the project … now we have the technology …

One: If you have all the technology, then why don't you just create a paradise?

Maestro: That's exactly what we want to do! But it can be done only if we can unlock people's mind, change their perception and let them realize that their own slavery is the source of misery!

Psychiatrist: We have to get them out from under the deadly control that paralyzes the potential energy that would be otherwise the driving force of society!

Steve: Right on! Yayaya! This whole thing might sound naive and banal to you, but the pure fact that you are here now must be convincing enough that we are heading to the right direction!

Andy: I'm not convinced at all … I have never been convinced about anything.

Marilyn: I feel rather suicidal under all this pressure you are putting on us … I wish I was dead again …

Three: But what if they are actually right?! What if we can do it?! Wouldn't you be happy to help out the whole world for a big change?

Four: The biggest thing since the Big Bang!

One: Theoretically I'm in … but what do we have to do exactly?

Steve: Finally you asked the most important question …

Psychiatrist: Exactly! How to do it! …

Maestro: I want to quote another ghost … the question is now: "What has to be done?"

Four: All right Comrades! Let's forget for a moment all the conceptual bullshit and theoretical clichés ! So what you want us to do?!

Steve: Right on! Here we go! Yayaya!

Psychiatrist: Amen!

One: The Earth might not be the centre of the Universe, but we are!

3/ They are sitting around a table that is empty now.

Maestro: Most importantly and first of all you'll have to engage yourselves in sexually intense performances during the next few days.

One: Aha, so that's why you selected me, a dead porn star.

Maestro: Exactly! You have a very important part in this production! We'll gang bang you in order to increase the power of your brain waves which will carry part of the messages to the masses of people around the world … during sexual extasy the radiation of the brain radically multiplies, the waves' amplitudes are much stronger and each oscillation can carry more complex messages.

Andy: I don't mind watching but I can't really provide my body directly … I'm so shy …

Psychiatrist: We know that, Andy. You are here because of your iconic place in art history as the king of pop-art. People are familiar with your art works such as the Campbell soup series or your portraits of superstars and they can also easily recognize your face because of your particular look ... we need your brain waves to break into the frequency fields of their collective memories

Andy: I never thought I had any brain waves, I always felt so empty ... are you sure I am the right person? I'm so shy ...

Maestro: No worries, Andy. We know you are shy ... it's part of the script.

Two: Do you know that I'm epileptic?

Psychiatrist: Of course ... that's why you are here.

Maestro: During epileptic seizure an eruption like electric discharge occurs that would be impossible to produce otherwise ... this explosive force will be one of our devices for the success of the transmission

Three: Convulsion as a weapon! And who are the ones to be sacrificed?

Psychiatrist: The bad news is that all of you, yes, by the end of this experiment you'll all have to die for the 2nd time. I'll make sure you'll die in peace.

Four: I just started having some good time and I'm looking forward to have sex ... Can we make a deal that you would let us exist afterwards?

Maestro: But you are dead ... You must understand, only this very specific, supernatural location gives you the illusion that you are alive ... would you like to stay in this prison for ever? Perhaps you could ... but the moment you leave you cease to exist again.

Two: No escape.

Steve: It's impossible! But what you'll accomplish will be the greatest event in history! You'll change the whole world, you'll be heroes!

Three: Please stop this patronizing talk. Just tell us what to do and we deal with the rest.

Four: Doesn't this sound so simple!? Some sex and convulsion and the world becomes a paradise!

4/ Sex scene and convulsion

They gang bang **One**, various poses. **Two** is convulsing accompanied by others. As their sex and seizure activity is going on they are watching the news on a cell phone and learn about a series of revolutions progressively developing all around the world

Steve: That's amazing! I can't believe it! It's happening almost everywhere … Let's fuck your brains out! More and harder, let's that transmission succeed. More convulsions please! … The world is on fire, revolutions everywhere, people are taking over, we are doing it, yes, it's unstoppable … sex and technology are working together against authoritarian systems …Hallelujah!

Everyone is fucking and convulsing in the room …

5/ The Maestro is sleeping alone on a bench … He wakes up. Slowly sits up.

Maestro: It's not so easy to be a ghost. Sometime things work out sometime not. But I love this old prison and I want to stay here for a while. I died in prison so I'm used to it. What's going to happen in the world after this revolution I have no idea. I'm not even sure if it was real … I used to think that sex was the driving force of society and I still convinced it is but ganged up with technology. By the way, before I would say good bye to you I would like to introduce myself. My real name is Wilhelm Reich. I mean I'm the spirit of Wilhelm Reich.

MANIFESTO ART CRAP RIOT

WHO HAS THE AUTHORITY TO DETERMINE WHAT IS GREAT ART AND WHAT IS CRAP? WHO HAS THE AUTHORITY TO JUDGE WHAT IS AN IMMORTAL MASTERPIECE AND WHAT IS IMMATURE JUVENILE PIECE OF SHIT?! THE CRITICS? THE MUSEUMS? THE CORPORATIONS? THE BANKS? THE RENTAGON? BROADCAST IMPERIALISM? I HAVE FOUGHT AGAINST THE DOMINATION OF CORPORATE POWER AND I HAVE FOUGHT AGAINST INSTITUTIONAL DOMINATION, AGAINST SHINYISM. I HAVE CHERISHED THE IDEAL OF FREE EXCHANGE OF IDEAS AND FREE COMMUNICATION FOR EVERYONE. I REFUSE TO LEAVE THE TECHNOLOGY OF CREATIVITY AND COMMUNICATION IN THE HANDS OF THOSE WHO CONTROL IT FOR THEIR OWN PROFIT. I REFUSE TO BE OPPRESSED BY THEM. I REFUSE TO LEAVE THE MASS MEDIA STRICKTLY TO THE OTHER GUYS. IT IS AN IDEAL WHICH I HOPE TO LIVE FOR AND TO ACHIEVE. BUT IF NEEDS BE, IT IS AN IDEAL FOR WHICH I AM PREPARED TO DIE!

Monty Cantsin

MESSIAH

In October 1994
you'll be in the mountains
take long walks
enjoy the fresh air
enjoy the fresh air
And surrounded by a dying nature
you'll meditate on death
you'll make a decision how you
would like to end your life
You want to blow up yourself
using a micro time bomb
that you can swallow easy
just like a vitamin pill
You want to be alone
in a sailboat
in the middle of the ocean
and when you swallowed down the pill
you'll jump into the water
and swim until
the redeeming explosion comes

The main intention of my life has never been fulfilled.
The main intention of my life should never be fulfilled.
Because the main intention of my life is to never be fulfilled.
Thus the main intention of my life is fulfilled.

I'm standing on a flying iron
and holding my body against the wind
I live among the angels of despair
my heaven is the abyss of nothing
Glory and stain
loss and gain

fame and shame
are all the same
Let's go blindly to disaster.
Return to the roots of desolation.
Cross the surface of dead illusion.
Enter the state of total zero.
The final place the game leads to is nothing.
I'm standing on a flying iron
and holding my body against the wind.

I have too many things to tell you but I don't know how to begin.
It's really difficult because you are very critical and you take
everything very seriously. If you were here and I could look
at your eyes it would be much easier, you know, because
when I look at you it feels like I was part of your body.
Like I was you and you were me. And then I could tell you
everything without saying a fucking word.

I'm standing still and I'm pointing to a white, empty wall.
I'm standing still and I'm pointing to a white, empty wall.
I'm standing still and I'm indicating my finger to head,
I'm standing still and I'm indicating my finger to head.
I'm doing it because it is futile.
I'm doing it because I believe it is futile.
I'm doing it because I believe that everything is futile.
I'm doing it because I believe in everything that is futile.
And I want to show that everything is futile.

All night long I can feel
the broken glass in my stomach
All night long I can hear
the rush of blood in my cerebral arteries

First of all you have to take a deep breath.
That's how everything always begins.
We are marching hand in hand
up to the monument: a huge pile of shit.

We all have the same dream
dream about an ice cold shower.
The meaning is standing behind
behind the shower curtain.
It is physically impossible to observe
a system without interfering
with the observed system itself.
Nothing is really happening
As we're given more and more,
more and more images to spit at
we run the increasing risk
of spitting at nothing at all.

The Lamb that was slain
the Lamb is the bad breath
the Lamb that was slain
the Lamb is the black river
the Lamb that was slain

the Lamb is the smoky sky
the Lamb that was slain
the Lamb is the greedy furcoat
the Lamb that was slain
the Lamb is the void of stupidity
the Lamb that was slain
the Lamb is the blood of corruption
the Lamb that was slain
the Lamb is the killing lie

I am the centre of the Universe
I feel the heavy dust pressing my eyes
I am the centre of the Universe
I feel the heavy dust burning my eyes
I live in an uncertain situation
that stimulates confusion, chaos
and disintegration
The continual failure is

the root of my success
I feel absolutely free
I feel absolutely free to be
absolutely free to be fucked up
I have no taste
I have no state
I have no estate
I'm fed up with the endless humiliation of
playing safe
I negate to negate the negation of negation
I negate to negate the negation of negation
Existence is not a necessity
Survival is annihilation
I can guarantee that nothing will turn out all right.
Everything will remain just as fucked up
as it has always been.
No oki, no doki.
The siren shall sound
And the dead shall be dead
and we shall be wiped out
and never say for ever
never say for ever
Amen.

I first performed Messiah on March 4, 1992, at the Music Gallery, in Toronto, as part of "The Anti-Cycles of Megaphony" voicegun-recital, with Brian Damage sampling/keyboard and Krista Goddess scrapmetal.

to the attention of
Shirley Thompson
director
The National Gallery of Canada
OTTAWA

jan 30, 1991

IDEAL GIFT
LETTER OF DONATION

reby declare that I donate a blood painting, int
:AL GIFT, to The National Gallery of Cani
ıwa, on jan 30, 1991. To create *IDEAL GIFT* I ł
d 6 vials of blood, taken from my arm. My dona
ıdes an additional interpretation to *IDEAL (*
led *SWEET BLOOD OF A DEAD PIGI*
NIFESTO, as well as supplementary informa
ut *Blood Campaign.*

With great expectations

AMEN.

SWEET BLOOD
OF A DEAD PIGEON
MANIFESTO

additional interpretation to *IDEAL GIFT*
jan 30,1991

It is not the first time that I waste my blood in museums and art galleries in order to demonstrate a desperate effort to avoid self-censorship and corruption at all costs.

IDEAL GIFT is the latest product of Blood Campaign, a continuous and long term project I have been doing for the past twelve years.

At many and various occasions, and especially in times of social crises Blood Campaign successfully proved the fact that any art which shows the repression of our society is automatically suppressed.

The function of Blood Campaign is to subvert culture, to question the very validity of established culture that is always corrupted by profit and controlled by censorship, to question the order of priorities, and especially the fact that property always seems to have priority over people and people's lives and needs.

As I'm reading this manifesto, thousands are being killed by the greedy, corrupt and murderous machinary of total censorship: war.

The aim of this blood painting is:

a
to make a dramatic statement
by radicalizing an empty white wall with the simple means of a symbolic gesture.

b
to create a critical open-situation that is both,
an impulse for communication in a repressive social reality
and a conceptual work of art that negates repression.

c
to signal an absolute alienation
from the ruling value systems of the post-modern cultural establishment
and the related business/military political-complex.

That's it for now. You have the option either to leave IDEAL GIFT on the wall until it becomes meaningless and obsolate, or eliminate it immediately with the very powerful disinfecting cleansing liquid of Mr. Clean.

What time is it?
AMEN.

National Gallery of Canada, Ottawa, Marcel Duchamp Room, Jan 30, 1991,
captured by Krista Goddess

National Gallery of Canada, Ottawa, walkway to freight elevator, Jan 30, 1991,
captured by Krista Goddess

EXCERPTS FROM

THE LAMENTATIONS OF ISTVAN KANTOR

In which a survivor mourns over the desolations brought on the City of Trans-missionaries and the Unholy Land of the Antenna Tribe by Broadcast Imperialism—Unauthorized version.

(He takes a deep breath and begins:)

I deconstruct the subject to confuse the readers just like I do it in my video works. I like to jump from one idea to another without being concerned with narrative continuity and the viewers' expectations.

It's again an autobio crime-anthem, a spit-psalm, expressing my struggle of daily survival and illegal activities under the demolishing conditions of technological society. Technology is necessary but to get ripped off by those who control it for their own profit is not. In a world that is ruled by enormous authoritarian systems, global organizations, mammoth-corporations, mega-businesses and government institutions, how can a small scale radical zombie, a non-institutionalized individual robot, an independent media-vamp and transmission machine, who is also a Neoist insurgent, like me, survive?

The mainstream perception of time is linear. Only those living on the edge, above the tumultuous abyss, like me, can perceive that we live in a non-linear world. Past, present and future are not separated. They are happening at the same time. In fact today's all determining equation is: past=present=future. It's just as scientific as it is a poetic notion. It's always six o'clock. The clock stopped at 6? Is it the bright arrow of the sun? Is it the y from the xy coordinates?

Let's not get too excited: the vertical arrow of 6 o'clock is only a visual illustration of the emergency signal of a new perception: an accumulating mess of information. Everything happens simultaneously, at the same time, at 6 o'clock. From the accumulating mess of information we can freely and openly pick anything we want. Plundering past, present and future, that's how we contemplate and that's how we time-travel. It's like growing up in a prison cell.

(Looks at the audience and laughs)

The idea of simultaneity in an Eden of sensory immediacy was a rosy psychedelic wet dream of hippies and all others repressed by the one-dimensionality of industrial society. But way before them surrealists and dadaist criminals attempted to counter and destroy the institutionalization of art and merge it with everyday life, unfreezing the power of dissent and revolt. Although this attempt fortunately failed (failed revolutions stay uncorrupted), subsequent avant-gardes had similar aims. But such revolutionary concepts of the 70s as "Everything is art" and "Everybody is an artist" today are old-fashioned, cliché-like slogans, common places.

Recently I was really surprised to hear that radicalism is back. Hmm, I said, that's great. I won't be so lonely anymore …

(Hahaha from the audience)

Since political correctness took over and radicalism was ousted, art is a mere entertainment for the government controlled elites and it has lost its social and political values. The dominant institutional elites divert people's attention from collective struggles to cultivate the artist's image as a polite individual quietly gardening the soul of art lovers and massaging the heart of museum visitors while selling jars of marinated squids and calamaris for hundred million$. No confrontations, no crises.

All supposedly challenging counter-artistic practices—anti-art, non-art, anti-aesthetic, seemingly non-institutionalizable forms of permanent revolt—are quickly and oppressively institutionalized, gobbled up by the ravenous institutions of official art. But remember video was supposed to be a confrontational tool through the instant information it could provide. The first time I got a video camera in my hands, around the late 70's, I used it to watch myself masturbating. That's how I fell in love with video and became an addict. And my fascination with technology is just as strong today as it was then. However my opinion about the system that provides and controls this technology has changed and evolved just like my vocabulary. Fuk da system!

(More hahahas)

Radicalism in art, radicalism as a form of expression, has been absorbed and taken over by the institutional culture. As a matter of fact the Marina Abramovic show at the MoMA has been a clear statement about that. Is this the victory of pure critical radicalism or is it a complete tribute to Broadcast Imperialism? Will the MoMA invite me one day to re-enact my 1988 blood-intervention "GIFT" and officially recreate my illegal blood-X on the wall between two Picassos? Will I be permitted to splash some blood on one of the Picassos (*Girl with Mirror*) without being charged with $10 million in damages? Or maybe I'll be paid $10 million to do it? And above the front entrance of the MOMA will they hang a huge banner saying: "I refuse any and all authority from institutions, judges and establishment idiots!" Signed: Monty Cantsin open-pop-star?

Gentrification has not only cleaned up the cities' abandoned buildings but it also resulted in a new ideology that I call shinyism. In my iconic world, in the dystopian homeland of Totalitaria, that is the location for a post-neo-Orwellian hyper-pulp heimat-novel, shinyism operates through Broadcast Imperialism under the control of the Rentagon in Retropolice (capital of Totalitaria) with King Realtor sitting at the head of the table in the MonoPolitburo's Bored-room.

Let's give the mic to King Realtor!

(He continues the narration as King Realtor:)

"It's very obvious that the shiny screen of television, computer and cell phone represent today's mainstream communication system. Everyone around the world is subject to these everyday tools of technology. When you sit in front of a computer screen you are looking right into the mirror of shiny-ism. That bright screen not only reflects the shinyist ideology but it sucks you in.")

(Voice from the audience: fuck King Realtor, just be yourself!)

(He looks toward the direction of the voice and then goes on:)

Yes, I agree, fuck King Realtor! The reality of shinyism became completely evident by the early 00s. This is basically old news, no explanation needed. It becomes a bit more complicated when we learn that we are all controlled by the global power of Broadcast Imperialism (BI) and the control system of BI is based on methods of gentrification. I use the term gentrification in a broader sense than just real estate's condominium business extravaganza. I don't simply mean the demolishing of old buildings and construction of new ones, or the eviction of poor people replaced by virtuous yuppies. I base my logic on the following enumeration:

GENTRIFICATION – EVICTION – EXTERMINATION – GENOCIDE.

I'm talking about the gentrification of all aspects of life including people's brain. Twenty-four hour mind-blinding and brainwash through shinyism. This is one of the most radical changes that happened to the world since World War Two. The shiny virus of digital gentrification (wrongly called digital revolution) infested the whole world. Everything has been gentrified through the shinyist ideology of Broadcast Imperialism. Including prisons and museums. Both institutions are now made from the same construction blocks of shinyism (including people's blood mixed into the chrome-concrete).

Prison=Museum. Is this a surprise? No. It's easy to understand if we just examine the main characteristics of these institutions. These are: *high security, surveillance and permanent collection.* Both institutions are equipped with the newest devices of high technology.

The shiny screens in the offices are serving the system with total control. They are all connected through the global network. Once this was a dream known as "global village"… but now it's a nightmare.

(Voice from the audience: Your nightmare!)

Yes, true, like most criminals I live in a world of nightmares. After being banned for almost two decades from the National Gallery of Canada, I recently took the Gallery to court and, backed by a law firm and a criminal defence lawyer, I won my case based on constitutional rights and freedom of speech. At the same time I lost my trial vs the Hamburger Bahnhof—Museum für Gegenwart (Museum for the Present) in Berlin for defacing the wall with my blood next to Paul McCarthy's gold Michael Jackson statue. But my fine and expenses were paid by a local gallery owner who followed my work with sympathy for a number of years. In 2006 the Art Gallery of Ontario banned me from its premises for the second time within 20 years for creating a blood-intervention "Deadly Gift" in front of Andy Warhol's *Red Disaster*. As an additional result all my work-in-progress projects with the AGO were suspended. In nov/2008 I hit the Hamburger Bahnhof for the second time, but this time I used a picketing sign in front of a giant Joseph Beuys quotation "Die Revolution Sind Wir" (We are the revolution) at the Beuys retrospective. On my banner I added: Und Wir Auch (And we also). I was arrested again but I never showed up in court.

(Both boos and hahahas)

These are only a few examples of my most recent criminal records.

Now I'm asking you my dear robotic zombies, in times of shinyism when the leaders the global powers are parading in your town creating $billion bills while you can't even pay for your no-budget production costs, will you have the courage to confront them as a media-guerilla by pointing your video camera to their head? Do you really want to get beaten up, your camera broken, go to jail, fight at court, and your fingerprints and picture taken to become part of the Potential Terrorists' Files? Do you want to have a little note in your police record that will make your next trips to the G20 countries impossible?

(Voice from the audience: Our electronic fingerprint ID-s are circulated in shared police-files all over the world anyway!)

Let me conclude that neither a small scale clandestine solitary media activist, like a victim of police brutality in a big city, nor a professional mega-subversive hacktivist who enjoys public recognition everywhere in the world, has basically any chance to survive without cooperating with the Rentagon's leading establishment, without getting corporate support from Broadcast Imperialism, or just a little help from friends in the business of authority and power. Vicious campaigns of police intimidation to silence protestors everywhere and menaces by top politicians urging the assassination of internationally known political activists are part of the daily media events.

Therefore if today's young emerging media-star artist wants to make a successful career, then what does she/he have to do? Disguised as Wi-fi laptop soldier, after finishing college and/or university must get involved right away with corporate businesses assisted by a commercial gallery, a number of museums of contemporary art, funding institutions, banks, curators, publishers and collectors. Contrarily to this trendy emerging supernova model-character, the submerging outmoded fuck-off artist is unable to follow the rules. With fewer and fewer future perspectives, he/she is stubbornly cherishing romantic ideas about being a solitary warrior, keeping distance from the institutional politically correct cowardice-mechanisms and the standardized cliché-expectations of the art world. His/her reward for life achievement is an epitaph: Remembered in verses of poetry as a Halloween freak crowned with a wreath of fire, an abandoned false-prophet holding a sign "Resistance is Futile", a bleeding ghost from May 68 lying on the ground next to a broken Sony Portapak, an underground rebel buried in a luxury condominium's low level parking lot, described by McLuhan as "the antenna of the race", a fallen star hidden in the accumulating mess of overcrowded 6 o'clock Empire: disappeared without any trace.

(Cut to black)

NEOISM MANIFESTO

neoism has no manifesto

KRONONAUTIC DIVECTOR FIELD
CENTRE RECHERCHE NEOISTE
BOX 382 BALTIMORE M D 21203 USA (301) 659-7218

THE NEOISTS ANNOUNCE THAT A RESEARCH CENTER
HAS BEEN SET UP IN BALTIMORE, MARYLAND, US/A
IN SYMBIOSIS WITH THE KRONONAUTIC DIVECTOR FIELD. +
THE FORMATION OF BALTIMORE CENTER HAS BEEN
OFFICIALLY REPORTED TO A LARGE PUBLIC ON DEC 9 1980
AT PRATT CENTRAL OF BALTIMORE PUBLIC LIBRARY.
AFTER THE INAUGURATION THE ASSEMBLED NEOISTS
CELEBRATED ALL NIGHT AT DIFFERENT PLACES
IN BALTIMORE CITY. A DECISION HAS BEEN MADE
THAT THE APT '81 FESTIVAL WILL BE HELD
IN MONTREAL AT THE PEKING POOLROOM IN FEB 1981.

+ & OTHERS..

POR EKZAMPLO:
THE NEOISTS/KRONONAUTS/WHATEVERS ANNOUNCE:
THAT AN /OFF/ CENTRE DE RECHERCHE NEOISTE
AS BEEN ESTABLISHED IN BALTO. MD, US/A
IN SYMBIOSIS WITH THE KRONONAUGHT/T)Y
DIVECTOR FIELD KTP.. THE FORMATION OF
THE BALTO CENTRE AS BEEN
REPORTED 2 THE PUBLIC AT BALTO'S CENTRAL PUBLIC
LIBRARY. AFTERWORDS
THE NEOISTS/KRONONAUTS/WHATEVERS
ANNOINTED THEIR INTERIORS COPIOUSLY ALL NITE
IN DIFFERENT DIVECTOR FIELDS IN BALTO CITY.
A D CISION AS BEEN MADE THAT THE APT '81 FEST
WILL B HELD IN MONTREAL IN THE PEKING POOLROOM
IN FEB '81.

FOTOX:KOFERENCE.A BEJELENTES A KONYVTARBAN

b o pox 382, balto, md, 21203, us(a), earth

NURSERY RHYME

ART IS NOTHING
ART IS DEAD
ART IS LIVING
ART IS BREAD
ART IS JUNK
ART IS DUST
ART IS USELESS
ART IS A MUST
ART IS A BLOODY SON OF A BITCH
ART IS FOR THE POOR
ART IS FOR THE RICH
ART IS FOR YOUR EYES
ART IS IN YOUR HANDS
ART IS THE STORES
ART IS IN THE BANKS
ART IS SHIT
ART IS NADA
ART IS STUPID
ART IS BLABLABLA
BLABLABLABLABLABLA
ART IS HEAVEN
ART IS HELL
ART IS EVERYTHING
ART IS EVERYWHERE

Computer graphics Boris Wanowitch

ACCUMULATION – CONCEPT

We are flying over Totalitaria. It's difficult to see anything, not only because of the bad weather but also because the situation has changed and the spectacle is now buried under its own production. Someone might discover archeological sites of previous diplomatic systems like communism, fascism and democratism, and might hear the obscure and noisy sub-frequencies of perishing technological societies. In Totalitaria everything happens at once, at the same timelessness, at six o'clock. Here the most modern is the most archaic and the beautiful lovers of the future are the newly demolished public monuments. Because we can't emphasize enough on the confusing aspect of vertical reality (symbolized by the two-sided vertical arrow of six o'clock) that opposes linear progression, we begin this trans-poetical adventure with an emergency landing over the Lake of Death.

***

In a decaying world the only real thing is the moment of death. Death, just like birdshit, is essential to increase the production of accumulation.

***

After the emergency landing that basically turned into a disastrous crash, increasing the production of ruins, the first thing we learn is that there is no such thing as linear progression measured by time. It would be more spectacular to say that time is dead but how could I say such a stupid thing when I know that, in the first place, time has never existed. I base this statement on my own poetical research rather than on second hand scientific truth, like the theory of Julian Barbour for example, and I don't intend to back it up or prove anything. But, if life presents itself as an immense accumulation of spectacles, as I read somewhere a long time ago, then this accumulation is the measure of life. Everything that is directly lived must move into this accumulating and massive timeless mess that can only expand vertically. There is no beginning, no progress, no end. There is only accumulation. It's always six o'clock.

***

Vertical reality can be considered both an object of mere contemplation and a theory with objective facts of reality. Decay and ruins are the concrete testifying elements of this immense multilayered accumulation where truth can not be presented through the lies of science. The lies of science can include a large scale of ideas but I have no intention to be more specific. Let's just mention that the different theories of time (Copernicus, Newton, Einstein) were part of the lies. But from now on the lie of time has lost its value just like all art objects accumulated in museums all around the world that were valued by signatures and dates. No time, no history, no art. I repeat: it's always six o'clock in Totalitaria.

***

In vertical reality everything happens at once, simultaneously. Accumulation presents itself as a massive field of unification with no beginning and no end. But as things are accumulating they also get alienated from their original functions and thus separated from their history: the ruins of separation in the field of unifying decay.

***

Accumulation is not a collection of history, images, objects, ideas, but an expanding field of vertical reality that integrates everything without exception. In Totalitaria the Great Confusion rules.

***

Accumulation can be understood as a vextatic earritainment and abusement of the spectacle of noise, as a product of post-historical technological society. Ideas accumulating in the messy field of vertical reality are dated and futile. The spectacle of noise is objectified by the meaningless accumulating mess that has no value whatsoever other than confusion. The spectacle is not visible as spectacle only the accumulated gigantic mess of the spectacle manifests itself through noise.

***

Accumulation is the result of the production of everyday life. It is life itself without the measuring force and authority of time. It is a mass of confusion composed of information, history, objects and people. Accumulation is a continuous and ongoing process that will never be interrupted by any means of culture, economy or politics, in other words the spectacle of noise. In fact the spectacle is buried under the accumulated noise that makes up this multi-layered mass that is all. It's very simple and easy to understand once we agreed that there is no such thing as time.

***

Accumulation represents the unity of the world. In the mass of accumulation there is no difference between image and reality. In other words in vertical reality history, mythology and present reality are the same things. They all exist together, simultaneously, as part of a total system. In this total system nothing can be separated but all things are connected to each other. The language of the spectacle is noise: the sound of confusion: the unity of Totalitaria.

***

Accumulation is the only result of the spectacle of noise that sums up the different forms of social activities. These activities are divided by the smaller systems of production but that doesn't change the outcome: everything gets absorbed by the mass of accumulation and becomes part of the same unifying system of accumulation. Accumulation exterminates the spectacle.

***

The concept of accumulation simplifies but also confuses the great diversity of the spectacle of noise. The interconnections among the different systems are multiplying and forming networks and sub-networks. The accumulated information is stored in the networks' information storage hardware, including computers and furniture. Digitally accumulated information circulates through the Internet and gets manipulated, reused, recycled. The spectacle of noise is the affirmation of all information accumulated in the networks, regardless the content or quality of the information. It's just a big mess that keeps expanding in the virtually expanded vertical reality, escaping the need of timing devices. Clocks are only useful in timebombs.

***

The spectacle of noise is an ongoing festival that needs no description as it includes everything from birth to death. This is why I can say just any bullshit without worrying about making a statement that makes sense. My language is part of the spectacle of noise and thus it describes it through its own structure. What I'm trying here is to restructure what already has been said millions of times by people in the streets, in restaurants, in bedrooms, in offices. I'm just having fun with words that are so functional in negating linear progression and time.

***

Accumulation presents itself as something enormous, a huge mess of information accessible and inaccessible at the same time. Basically it's all the same shit, it only appears to have different parts and segments. It's there, it can be used or ignored. To deal with it, and to survive in Totalitaria, it's better to have a good sense of humour, hyper-absurd and ultra-poetical.

***

In Totalitaria the sun never sets. There is no beginning and no end. Accumulation is the only meaningful process of life. In fact I probably overrate its importance. I overrate the importance of words as well when I say that my ideas cover the entire surface of the world and I bath endlessly in my own accumulating shit.

***

Accumulation is not the result of control but the result of timeless decay. Accumulation has no goal. Its only measure is its vertical expansion. Therefore this is a useless theory that aims at nothing other than itself, like sucking your own cock and licking your own cunt. We are getting close to the idea of fuckoff revolution that is the permanent event of Totalitaria.

***

Accumulation requires specific methods of production/reproduction in order to save what is discarded by the false reality (rationality) of the system of decay. The spectacle of noise poses an emergency situation where triggering interactions through the sirens of necessity is the answer to all sectors of production, economy, politics, culture, religion, etc.

***

Accumulation does not present any obligation to reality, it's reality that can't escape the process of accumulation. But as accumulation is a must, it represents an oppressive force that challenges society. The constant noise of the system is a signal of warning that keeps in mind the need for insurrections.

***

The domination of accumulation over progress sets the ambience of noise in Totalitaria. The accumulated shit accompanied with champaign glasses and blood tubes is the ultimate mass-media of culture in the age of vertical reality. Perhaps flaming irons, coat hangers, black and red flags, file cabinets, refrigerators, megaphones and many other objects can be mentioned here for philosophical distraction and for the sake of theoretical demoralization of serious thoughts. This immense mess, shaped by gravity, must collapse into its own vacuum of freedom or revolve around its own axis causing avalanches in social reality and shaping the world of communication.

***

Who cares about the accumulation of shit anyway? Is there any interest of business in this pseudo-theory of poetical contemplation? At certain moments, mostly during wars and revolutions, when worlds are collapsing faster and turning into instant-rubble, the process of accumulation can be sensed better even by those who would never pay any attention to the spectacle of noise. Seeing and hearing what's happening in the living rooms or in the streets is not a privilege but a routine of daily rituals, except for those who are limited in functional sensorial organs. But even those can't escape the news as the logical systems of translation machinery obligate them to learn all the accumulating messages.

***

Philosophizing about vertical reality is not my job that would degrade me into a tired worker, but my amusement that recreates me into an anti-social idler or a criminal. If I only do what I like to do then I can accept my way of living as a philosophical statement. If I accept the theory of accumulation as the base of my philosophy of living then I would have to follow my theory which is more or less impossible because by accepting it I would push myself into self-oppressive authority of rules. Therefor accumulation can never take over my brain, my body or my office, it can only occupy the fields of everyday life to which I am superior.

***

Though through the power of philosophy I can reconstruct the world, the theory of accumulation in vertical reality will never change anything. In fact it can be applied to the past without erasing or changing the past, without any effect on anything. I'm not in and I'm not out. I'm just tied to myself integrating the negation of myself. That's how accumulation is perfected in my individual system.

***

The accumulation of dreams as a psychological dilemma has been already researched by scientists and artists and the result was summed up in one short phrase of wisdom that sounds something like that: making a living while accumulating debts is a nightmare. However if the sun never sets in Totalitaria, as we lightheartedly reported above in a colourful statement, then there is no such thing as nightmare either. The nightmare section therefore, that has so much to do with the ultimate expression of misery and despair, can be conveniently eliminated from our memory or simply replaced with reality.

***

The uninterrupted course of accumulation is the central subject of this fragmented essay-monologue because I am convinced that accumulation is, was and always will be the most important phenomenon of existence. Accumulation is also my never realized phantasy self-portrait I imagined to paint as the visionary manager of Totalitaria. Of course while this poetical view of subjectivity makes it less or more unrealistic, the basic idea of the system of accumulation and its related machinery has been drawn up. I don't think it's necessary to be more exact as I'm not trying to prove anything that can be labelled scientific. The abolishment of time that is the necessary condition for vertical reality has been declared and that's more than enough to start a war. Further ideas concerning the subject will be developed according to the needs of mediation and the size of the cleavage it caused within Totalitaria.

***

Accumulation is the alpha and omega of the spectacle of noise. This noise is dominated by the independent movements of machines. The total system is made up of specific machineries seemingly separated from each other but always connected through various means of communication devices. Vertical reality is an ever-expanding field that can be compared to the commodity market where noise is made through economic control-machines.

***

While writing this text I was sitting in front of my computer, detached from the rest of the world, focusing on a subject that survives only in a critical field of interactive counter-philosophy. Of course when taking it to real life in order to test it as a practical tool no success can be predicted until the whole system responds to my appeal.

***

In the land of accumulation all activity remains activated causing continuous interventions, overlapping structures, sudden changes, global explosions, turmoil, tumult, turbulence. Everything happens at once and simultaneously. It's accumulation that makes the earth shake at six o'clock and demolishes the difference between art and life, labor and leisure. At one point all activity gets half-dissolved into the spectacle of noise only to re-explode over and over again and again. Voices of screaming varying in between orgasmic expressions and howls of misery add to the concert.

***

Due to the aggressive and total techno-takeover isolation has become seemingly impossible. No lonely crowds can be detected anymore, not even as family meetings or sex orgies. The toast of the father at Sunday dinner echoes through the neighbourhood via the old-fashioned community cable network. Sex partners are connected to digital systems, home computers and big screens, and the impulses for their erotic motions and satisfaction is generated by global interactivity. The accumulation of misery reunites youth in the streets to demonstrate the pure elegance of unity by getting naked and fucking their brains out in front of the Imperial Bank of Totalitaria. Meanwhile some reckless elements with a different taste for subversion and sabotage, dated radicals of the scum of society, make a failed attempt of putsch by setting the same bank on fire. But their real desire that undermines their consciousness, infiltrating their own mental system, is to rediscover the traditional meaning of isolation in post-Gulag prison cells.

***

It would be easy to go on and on, draw endless quantity of even more ambiguous pictures and make more indefinite poetical statements that make everyone feel uncomfortable in their own decaying body. However, as my goal is not to fulfill my ambitions as a creator but rather as a criminal element, I should stop sitting in front of the computer and get back to active intervention. The products of my life surrounding me in my office, a beautiful set visually interpreting the theory of accumulation, are just as much alienated from me as I am alienated from the whole society. Therefor I'm standing alone without any belongings and without belonging to anywhere.

***

The turmoil of accumulation ceaselessly grinds its own powerful image of capital. It's not anymore just sucking your own cock as leisure but biting it off as self-defence.

***

In the empire of accumulation nothing can be independent. The rubble, like the broken seconds, is part of the system and is not deleted from the functional matters of reality. It's always six o'clock, as we already made several notes of that above. Clocks are futile in Totalitaria. The clock industry is condemned to bankruptcy. After breaking your chains will you please also step on your watch. Thank you.

Puppet Government, 1999 Toronto

Photo Jowita Kepa

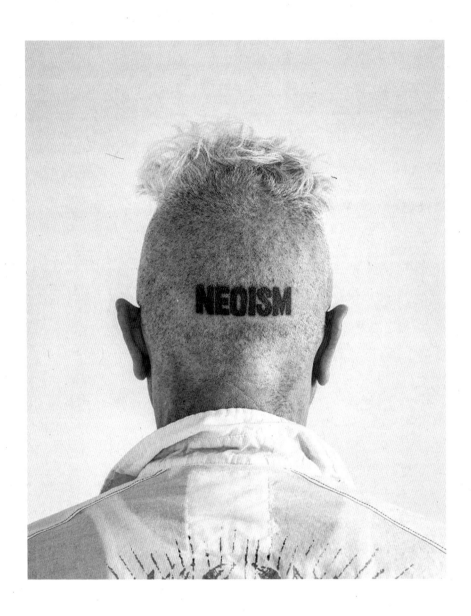

Photo Ariane Laezza 2017

(THE NEVER ENDING) OPERETTA
SHORTENED SCRIPT

Opening sequence of cinematic fiction and cliché news clip reality: image of the Earth from space. Spaceship moves by. Zoom into a 9/11 footage. War scenes. Religious protestors. Global Warming. Ice fields. Narrator's voice:

"The dawn of the 21ˢᵗ Century. The lust for global power had never been greater. Terrorism and military dictatorship rules the world dominated by Globalization. Alongside political and religious upheavals, the environment is also rising against its destroyers. Global Warming is the greatest threat to the planet."

Cut to an industrial section of Toronto, in the Bloor/Lansdowne area. Old warehouse buildings. Concrete cement trucks. Mix of past/present/future. Everyday life factory-scape. Train goes by. Strange looking people walk around. Police sirens. People running and screaming. Barking dogs. Marching band. Children playing in a courtyard.

Morning time. The sky is cloudy. Smoke is rising from a factory chimney. A car stops. A few men in business suits climb out. They are covering their noses with their hands. They slowly walk around looking at the buildings.

Old, worn out, squeaking garage door opens.
The Starving Artist steps out into the light. He is wearing a military looking jumpsuit with big letters on the back: STARVING ARTIST. He takes a deep breath and looks at the cloudy sky.

Three teenage kids walk out from behind him, through the garage door, a girl and two boys. They sit on their bicycles and say goodbye.

"Bye Daddy."
"Bye kids, ride carefully and have a great day at school."

He keeps waving his hand as they disappear on their bicycles.

A cement truck goes by and the driver waves hello to him. A cyclist, wearing an anti-pollution mask, also greets him. The men in business suits walk by, covering their noses.

The street now suddenly turns into a stage. The Starving Artist sings "*I Love The Stench*". The visuals reflect the content of the lyrics. It introduces the industrial section where the Starving Artist lives, an area that was saved from gentrification because of the heavy pollution, the constant bad smell and the accumulation of concrete-dust, caused by a jelly-factory and a concrete plant. The song evolves into an inflammatory speech like manifesto.

Telephone rings. The Starving Artist picks it up in his studio.

"*Hi, I'm calling from* The Star *for an interview for the City section. Can you tell me about what's it like to be an artist in Toronto?*"

"*The best thing about being an artist in Toronto is misery. My inspiration comes from misery. So for that reason I couldn't find a better place. Toronto is the post-Orwellian vampire capital of the incorporated dictatorial empire ruled by the Rentagon. Rents are extremely high, so are gas and electricity rates. I can't heat my studio in the winter.*"

"*And what do you like about your neighbourhood?*"

"*My favourite thing about this area is the stinking smell coming from the jelly-factory down the street and the accumulation of dust resulting from the concrete factory across from my studio. It keeps the developers away.*"

"*What do you think about Toronto's new cityscape?*"

"*I'm more interested in watching the street corner operas of everyday life. There are intense performances in my neighbourhood involving the passers-by, the drug dealers and the police. But the best visuals in Toronto were demolished anyway, and turned into vampire condos for fast profit. Toronto's cityscape is a disaster.*"

Nightmare sequence of Toronto cityscape. The architecture of the new buildings dominate the visuals of cinematic mayhem. The Starving Artist walks in the streets fenced up by the oppressive, monolithic prison walls of the condominiums. He suddenly becomes a lonely, lost, Charlie Chaplin like figure. Narrator sits in a café and looks out to the street. Narrator's voice:

"Now being a rare species of a soon to be extinct community, the Starving Artist is surrounded by a hyper-tech society living in luxury condominiums. Built on the grounds of demolished warehouses that were once the home of starving artists, these monolithic luxury condos are now the icons of Successful Living. They are also War Memorials, erected by the Rentagon, to commemorate the Final Victory of the Rich over the poor. But was it really their Final Victory?"

We see through the window of the café the Starving Artist joined by friends. He is now an activist. They are marching in the street. The march becomes a mass demonstration. The Starving Artist speaks. He is now a revolutionary speaker. He is arrested by the police. In jail for the night. He dreams about a revolution. The dream-like narrative video images tell about the events of the 2016 Toronto Revolution in the form of a dance-like piece of choreographic movement. The revolution is led by the Starving Artist against the forces of the Rentagon. It is an ironic theatrical performance of an imaginary heroic revolution. Narrator's voice:

"In 2016, the World's one and only multicultural city, Toronto, became the center of a worldwide uprising against the ruthless dictatorship of the Rentagon and its oppressive system of Broadcast Imperialism. High profit gentrification, homelessness and child poverty, police state terror, social and political abuse, tele-bureaucratic colonization, technological hyper-control were among the basic issues uniting the world's population into one rebel army. Millions joined the fight in the hope of a final victory over the many headed bloodsucking monster of Broadcast Imperialism. But history again failed to honour freedom over injustice. The revolution was crushed by the military forces of the UBIS – United Broadcast Imperialist States and the Anti-Terror Police of the Rentagon. Toronto, together with other rebel-cities, was wiped out and almost completely erased to the ground."

The spoken words are accompanied by music that creates the rhythmic flow of the images. The Starving Artist and his friends die in the battle, but their spirit survives forever. Narrator's voice:

"There was only one small place that miraculously survived the attack: The Break. The Break was an after hours cabaret located in the Queen West area. It was run by a group of artist-insurgents who were active in the uprising. They kept the place open throughout the revolution and even during the final disaster. While all the revolutionaries lost their lives on the barricades their spirit survived among the ruins. Inside the Break an endless party went on. Here in this decadent post-revolutionary cabaret, run by the Spirits of dead revolutionaries, survivors of the local population could visit the past, confront the present and experience the future simultaneously at once, like in a dream, by simply entering the premises that served as a user interface."

The Starving Artist appears on the stage and performs a song:

Hi!
I'm the guy from the Eastern Block Lunatic Asylum,
I fled the premises thirty years ago. Go!
I lived in Budapest, Paris, Montreal, New York,
A sexy prophetess led me to Toronto. Oh, oh, oh …

My children were born here in the 90's,
The struggle for survival set the family rules,
Food bank dinners, unpaid bills, protest marches,
Mike Harris theatre without applause.

Nothing happened to me by chance,
I was shaped by the experience.
My life style brought me here.
Nothing happened to me by chance.
Nothing! Nothing! Nothing!

I had been nurtured from youth
In an atmosphere of oppression.

I had known the totalitarian world
From inside the Iron Curtain.

I had broken the law,
I rot in prison cells,
I fought in the streets
And fled across frontiers.
Nothing happened to me by chance,
I was shaped by the experience.

Ladies and Gentlemen!
Being an artist of the controversial kind,
Being a single father of three,
Breaking the rules, refusing to bind,
Kept me in good shape,
And in good contact with poverty.
Nothing happened to me by chance,
I was shaped by the experience.

By the end of the song we are back in the industrial neighbourhood, in front of the garage door of the Starving Artist's studio. A neighbour comes to say hello to him.

"Did you hear that the concrete plant people lost their lease and they'll
soon be moving?"
"Then we'll be out of here soon too."
"I've had enough of this misery anyway."
"Unless we do something …"
"What would you like to do, start a revolution?"

They laugh. The Starving Artist turns and goes back to his studio.
He pulls down the garage door.

The group of men in business suits walk by again. One of them takes out a piece of paper from his briefcase and posts it on the garage door. They drive away. Close up on the post:

0

EVICTION NOTICE

Dear Istvan,

GET THE FUCK OUT FROM HERE!

THE RENTAGON

WHY IS A SIMPLE IDEA SO ASTONISHING?

WHY IS A FILTHY PRISON SO MAGNIFICENT?

WHY IS A DAMNED NOBODY SO DANGEROUS?

WHY IS A DEAD ARTIST SO FAMOUS?

WHY IS MY STINKY BODY SO ATTRACTIVE?

WHY ARE MY SWELLING VEINS SO INSPIRING?

WHY IS A STERILE NEEDLE SO DRAWING?

WHY IS A DROP OF BLOOD SO SIGNIFICANT?

WHY IS THIS BLOODY WALL SO POWERFUL?

WHY IS THIS PIECE OF SHIT SO PRECIOUS?

WHY IS MY MISERY SO FASCINATING?

WHY ARE THESE STUPID QUESTIONS SO BRILLIANT?

Stupid Questions Oct/1994

LETTERS TO SARENCO

sept 4, 1998 Toronto

Dear Sarenco,

finally here is a message from you, thanks, I thought we made a previous agreement about money and I was actually really counting on it for this month's budget, and now your fax makes me feel very uncertain about the whole thing and screws my present financials as well, it's a generous offer from you to present my work in your gallery and by giving me a solo exhibition in Italy you are really making history, but we agreed that you'll send me $5000 by the end of august and now you say you cannot do it because of your partners?, you'll pay me on the spot, you say, are you and your partners afraid that I would just keep the advance money and wont actually go?, I want to be very straight with you about this because I really need money for my survival and though I take risk all the time as an artist I cant do it as a self-employed producer, I have to make sure that I can pay my bills, feed my three kids and pay off my accumulating debts, otherwise I'm dead, it's a difficult task to be a subversive and in the same time expect money for it, but that's what NEOISM?! supposed to deal with, confusion, contradictions, misery, paradise, and so on, you know the game, I can only make it to Verona, if, in some form, I am assured of the outcome and dont have to worry about the financial parts, are you and your partners afraid that you cant sell my artworks and make money?, well, you proposed the exhibition at firsthand and you are in the gallery business, you must know what you can or can not sell, but $10 thousand for 30 artworks of Monty Cantsin is a great deal and that much I know as well, in two years nobody will be able to make any more artworks in this century that will end soon with Neoism and will be over for ever, and all the works produced in this century will cost a fortune, including the Monty Cantsins, as for the ticket: I can require information about the price here and let you know, so you can decide where it's less expensive, I like your gallery space and if we can fix the above problems I'll certainly be there on oct 4, can the walls be painted? or do they have to be white?, can you please look for some thrift stores, second hand stores where we can buy the necessary furniture material at my arrival, I'll need some help for the installation, I'll tell you more later, ciao Monty

***

sept 30, 1998

Dear Sarenco,
time is here to make some bloody plans for my crime in Verona including the broken furniture show in your gallery:

oct 4, sunday evening
Right after my arrival I want to see the headquarters(the gallery). We can also have a meeting, talk over things, take care of financials over a glass of wine, dinner, etc. Maybe some local conspirators can join us to talk about the possibility of a total take-over.

oct 5, monday
In the morning, after exercise and breakfast, at around 11am, I'll be ready to start terrorizing the city. You or someone else will take me to second hand furniture stores, thrift stores, junkyards, whatever places there are in Verona for buying or just finding used furniture. If we can find free stuff in the street it's even better, but probably Verona is not like a fucked up North American city with lots of junk all over the streets. Hopefully we can get all the shit together on monday and transport everything to the headquarters, I mean to your gallery. Meanwhile we also get some paint for the walls of the gallery. I'll decide about what look, color, sex, etc., exactly I want after seeing the place on sunday. We put the furniture in your gallery, and make a selection of them for each room. All this work has to be done by early evening, so we can have a good dinner, relax, enjoy the company of transsexuals and hyper-prostitutes, talk about revolution, sex, vandalism and whatever else comes to our mind.

oct 6, tuesday
I'll paint the walls. Hopefully there will be some lunatics to help me. We also might have to find more furniture. Early evening we can have some anti-social activity, blow up some buildings, set things on fire, etc. I would like to meet mafioso Francesco Konz for example (can be any day) and all the Neoists?! in Verona.

oct 7, wednesday
This will be the day of sexual assault on furniture. Perhaps someone can document it on video. I'll break everything. I'll need tools, like metal rod, hammer, saw, ax, pincers, wrench, and later lots of nails as well. Meanwhile I can talk to some stupid journalists, make some kind of a boring press conference and then kick them in the ass. Would be good to contact Politi at Flash Art, for example, he is a good idiot.

oct 8, thursday
I'll start arranging the mess, part of the shit will go on the walls, part of them will be damned on the floors. I'll bring some black markers, silver and gold markers, red and black peel-off china markers, etc., but probably I'll need some more, and will start adding icons, signs, etc., to each piece, until they look really bad.

oct 9, friday
I'll continue making a mess all day long until I get completely mad, can't take it anymore, shit on the floor, vomit all over the place and finally kill myself.

oct 10, saturday
Do the same bullshit as yesterday. Then cool down, take a cold shower, have a blow job, sign everything, give them titles. We'll set the lights and make it look like is was some kind of art exhibition.

oct 11, sunday
Opening. Tons of people, terrorists, mafia, prostitutes, dealers, and all the rest of misery. For my performance I'll make the final plans after my arrival because I don't want to make any plans that can not be done like in Mantova. For sure I want to have a nurse or doctor

for blood taking in 6 vacutainer vials, the kind that usually they use in hospitals.

I'll stay in Verona until oct 15 and so we will have three days to do some more subversion, create more riots, meet people interested in my criminal activities, take photos of the stabbed exhibition, etc.

The time has come, our laundry or death!

your immortal friend

Monty Cantsin

The Verona Crime, Oct. 1998, Sarenco, Club Art Gallery, photo Fabrizio Garghetti

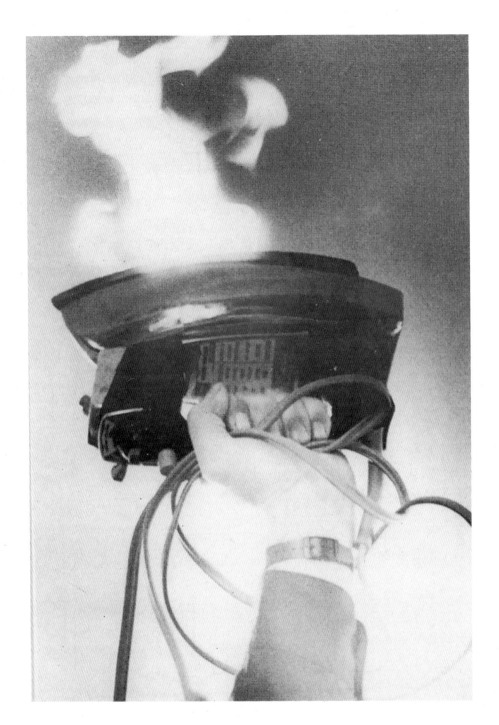

Photo Bretty Nova

THE FLAMING IRON

The image of ironing woman is one of the most common
cliche images of the life of the American housewife
ironing the white shirt of her American husband
This cliche image of the American housewife
represents the oppression of American women
Represents slavery

Now take an iron in your hand
If you are a real American man probably this is the very first time
you hold this strange object in your hand
Now take an iron in your hand
If you are a real American woman you probably never never never
never even want to touch it again
Now spread some rubber cement on the bottom of the iron
then ignite the highly inflammable fuel
and hold up the flaming iron

You are holding the torch of revolution!
You are holding the torch of liberty!
You are holding the torch of neoism!

Now imagine millions of people marching in the streets
holding up flaming steam irons in their hands
Now Imagine millions of people dancing in the streets
Holding up flaming steam irons in their hands

And afterwards when the flames are out
the burned rubber cement leaves a dark sticky coating
on the bottom of the iron so you can't use it anymore
to iron a white shirt
Keep it like this and put it on your altar
It looks beautiful!

TRANSMISSION MACHINE
SPOKEN WORD COMPONENT

I'm frightened and I'm ashamed of myself for being frightened. I'm ashamed of myself for becoming what I have never wanted to become. And that's why I am frightened. I've been a victim of technology for a long time but somehow I always had strength to resist the system of technology. But now it seems like I lost my life-long battle and my revolution has failed.

Ladies and Gentlemen,
Please let me tell you what happened. It might be a good learning experience for you and it might help me too to heal my troubled mind through confession therapy. I have lived for over 50 years now and I have seen life as it is. I have seen misery, pain, desolation, despair, destruction, fire, blood and everything else. I have been a soldier and a slave. For a couple of years I also worked as paramedic nurse in Budapest before going to medical university. And of course I have seen lots of people dying. Mostly ordinary people, common people who died of heart attacks, accidents, suicide … They didn't have the glorious death of heroes, they didn't have famous last words.

Many of them died in my arms. And as I looked into their eyes I saw not only fear but also confusion. They were frightened and confused and there was a question in their eyes: Why? Were they wondering about why they had to die? No. They knew one day they would have to die. So then what were they wondering about? Maybe they were wondering about who I was, this strange guy holding them at the very last moment of their life. I admit it must have been frightening. But I think what they were really wondering about was something else. I think they were wondering about why they had ever lived!

Annabel Chong, the amazing porn artist who once had sex with 251 men within about 8 hours, said in an interview that "SEX IS GOOD ENOUGH TO DIE FOR." I repeat: "Sex is good enough to die for."

But can I say that, "Art is good enough to die for?" Well, if art is sex and sex is art then art is good enough to die for. Or if art is revolution and revolution is art then art is good enough to die for as well. I want to live and die for art! If it doesn't make you horny it's not art!

I was always very curious about prison life. Once when I was in a high security prison, the guards and my prison mates thought I was a crazy person, some kind of mental product because even though they beat me up and sexually abused me I kept being friendly to everyone. I let them gang bang me in the shower or to punch my face until I was bathing in my own blood. For some reason my behaviour irritated them and soon I got transferred to a psychiatric institute. There I had to wear a red armband because I was considered a dangerous criminal and the red armband was a sign of dangerous criminals. And I've kept wearing it ever since.

Once, a very long time ago, maybe millions of years ago, I was a monolith. You know what a monolith is? It is a large cube, a single massive stone. It's also called *prima materia*. I was a very dark monolith, a black monolith. I radiated free signals. In other words I was a single standing transmission unit. I transmitted free information in different parts of the universe simultaneously at once. Because just like a subatomic particle that can be at least two places at the same time I was standing erect at several places at the same time. I was standing here on the Earth, and I was also on the Moon and on the Jupiter, and maybe elsewhere. I don't remember everything. But I know that I had transmitted free creative information and I played a principal role in initiating civilization.

Then I turned into a file cabinet. File cabinets are monolithic sculptural objects made to store information. How boring to be a file cabinet one can say. No, not at all. It was very exciting. I was filled with information most of the time but sometimes I was empty. People pushed thick files of information in my body, they were moving drawers in and out of my body, they stuffed me with their ideas. I was excited all the time, it was like a constant intercourse, a spontaneous orgasmic performance. And soon I got connected to other file cabinets all around the world through the electronic networks. People digitized all the information that was stored in me. They turned it into invisible numbers. And all the information that was stored in my body was sent to other file cabinets via the computer system. And on the other end they turned the digital information into hard copies again. They just kept making hard copies of everything. Therefore they needed more and more file cabinets. In spite of the dominating force of digital technology the information storage furniture industry is still growing, getting bigger.

As a file cabinet I became very interested in information society, in information systems. I learned a lot through experience again. I learned that there was information exchange at many different levels and that information production was under the control of a higher system of protection and surveillance. I learned that the flow of information wasn't free at all. I learned that information technology controlled the world through the broadcast systems. I learned that broadcasting became the most powerful system of global control.

Once I was known as Wilhelm Reich. I was a psychoanalyst; many of you probably heard of me. I was a student of Freud who was very interested in sexual behavior as part of his psychoanalytical research. But I went further than him. I summed up my theory in one short sentence: "Sex is the driving force of society." But my ideas were not welcomed by the political parties of those times. The communists kicked me out from the communist party and the Nazis burned all my books. I escaped to the United States where I continued my research. I became convinced that the universe was filled with pulsating bio-energy. I called it orgone energy. I observed that the human body was enveloped in this energy. When it wasn't then it was not healthy. I realized that I could heal people with orgone energy. I made orgone energy accumulators. These were boxes made of layers of organic sheets and metal sheets. They were big enough for a person to sit in it. The orgone energy cabinet accumulated orgone energy and radiated it to the person sitting inside the box. I only made a limited number of these furniture like orgone accumulators but I considered it a very successful experience. When I wanted to disseminate my ideas and distribute the accumulators, the US government intervened. History repeated itself. My books were burnt and my orgone energy accumulators were destroyed. I was arrested and I died in prison just about 50 years ago, 1957.

When I was Adolf Hitler I murdered millions of people. But I also made millions of people believe in me. They trusted me and followed my commands. I promised them the most powerful empire to ever exist on Earth. I achieved my power through broadcast technology, through broadcast radio. It was a very new and important invention. People were hypnotized by my voice through radio broadcast. That's how I disseminated Nazi ideology and created the Third Reich. I took the idea from Lenin who did the same thing with communism. He created communist ideology and the Soviet Union with the help of broadcast technology. And that's how politicians work today as well. Except that they have many new tools. I don't have to explain that to you. There is no political power without broadcasting power and no one has the authority of broadcasting without a reliable and closely co-operating political system.

I was six years old when the Hungarian Revolution happened. It was the greatest failed revolution ever and I was part of it. I somehow slipped out from the air raid shelter and I pointed my toy gun to a Russian tank from behind a tree. The tank stopped and a soldier jumped out. I ran back in the house and hid in the dark. They surrounded the block and were looking for the boy. Lots of little boys died in those days while playing heroic revolutionaries. I kept playing it throughout my life. Among the games I played the kicked out game, the being evicted game, and also the being banned, deported, arrested and jailed games. Ever since I moved to Toronto I became more and more interested in revolution. Ever since my arrival in Toronto my life became centred on gentrification. Toronto is a capital of the global empire of gentrification. The upgrading of neighbourhoods is a very trendy subject here. For many people it means the loss of living spaces, evictions, demolishing of buildings, relocation of people against their will. For others it means the final victory of real estate, luxury homes, new businesses and higher profit. But gentrification is not only about the city and the neighbourhoods.

It is about people's minds, the way they live and think. Everything has been gentrified not only the neighbourhood. The arts had been gentrified; the museum and galleries have been gentrified. The libraries, theatres, parliaments, the streets, subways, police stations, hospitals, the church, the beaches, the train stations and airports, they were all gentrified. Joseph Beuys's social sculpture was gentrified. Even the Eternal Network was gentrified.

And gentrification couldn't be done without broadcast technology. Broadcast technology is the driving force of gentrification. It's been already quite a few years that we've been staring at those shiny, bright, glossy, friendly pulsating displays, screens, monitors. Their hypnotic shiny power is undeniable and we've known that for a long time. Shinyism rules. I'm not telling you anything new here. We live under the dominating control of broadcast technology and we embrace it.

Why do you think the AGO is building a $400-million façade? It will be a monument of Shinyism, a gigantic shiny screen made from titanium and glass, a titanic glossy surface of command and control.

It will pull people inside the AGO like a magnet. And inside the AGO there will be more shiny art. Why do you think the AGO didn't want me to mix my blood into the new walls. I proposed to them that I would mix my blood and other people's blood into the walls to create an invisible monument that pays tribute to the slaves of the arts. That pays tribute to those who lived and died for art. And for sex and revolution. But my blood is too dark and the AGO didn't want my dark blood to be associated with their new shiny building. They want shiny art, like the new art of Damian Hirst. You know the famous British artist who recently made a human skull sculpture from $100-million worth of diamonds. And this sculpture will be exhibited in the most important museums around the world. And then it will be purchased for five hundred million or more by one of the unknown honorary members of global gentrification. It will become part of a prestigious collection of Shinyist art. Gentrification denies everything that is dark because it reminds them of the dark ages when there was no broadcast technology yet. Even dark chocolate is too bitter for them.

I wonder what happened to the $10 million in damages I caused in the Museum of Modern Art 20 years ago. In 1988 I was charged with a felony for causing $10 million in damages to a Picasso with a few drops of my own dark blood. Even though they cleaned it up with some warm water and a few cue-tips, the museum claimed $10 million in damages. Being considered an anti-art artist this $10 million in damages equals $10 million worth of criminal art or damage-art. If I can create $10 million in damages with a few drops of my blood, imagine how much more damage Damien Hirst can create with the power of $100 million worth of diamonds? It's evident that art in a gentrified society means nothing else than the creation of money from money.

You can't just mix together some dirt, dust, mud, blood, salt and water and call it art. The *prima materia* of today's shiny art is not just money, but money and the power of broadcast technology.

The intense processing of information generates lots of heat in my body. While my head is spinning my cooling system also works hard. I am a transmission machine. Like everyone else. I transmit heat, sounds, voices, I radiate light, and all kinds of other signals, psychotronic, telepathic, extrasensorial, and I also transmit biochemical substances. I transmit more or less information under different conditions. My information transmission becomes almost overwhelming during orgasmic function and almost incomprehensible during a revolution. During epileptic seizure the body's information production surpasses all limits.

Transmission machines like me are independent units only transmitting directly from one to another. However lately, with all the new technology furnishing our homes we are also part of the global broadcasting system. We are the ones who pay the rent to the techlords and keep the Rentagon in business. We are feeding the parasites so they can parasite us even more. It's no longer the legendary magician, the wonderful OZ, nor the control freak mighty Big Brother standing at the wheels of control. It's a global system of higher technology that operates through Broadcast Imperialism.

During the 80s I lived in Montreal and New York at once. It meant lots of traveling between the two cities. I usually took Czechoslovak airline. It was cheap, only $79 return. And on the plane they sold a bottle of vodka for only $1. And this wasn't all. The plane shook a lot and, because the seats were made from metal, the shaking was even more significant. Everyone had the fear of death that produced tons of adrenalin in our blood. We were all totally excited. Today the seats are very comfortable, duty free items are expensive, and there is that little glossy hypnotic screen in front of everyone deliberately obligating us to constantly stare at Shinyism.

The only time when I get away from the gentrifying shiny waves is when I'm in the park doing my daily exercises. I do yoga, stretching, push ups, sit ups, chin ups, I also run, sing, pray and meditate. I try to do it for at least two hours every day. I go to High Park or Trinity Bellwoods when I'm in Toronto. In New York it was the East River Park, in Montreal I went up to the mountain. When I'm on the road I always look for a park right after my arrival.

I have a payer: Anyu, Nagyi, Kati, Apuko, Apu … Anyu is my mother, Apu is my father, Nagyi is my grandmother, Apuko is my grandfather, Kati is my sister. They are all dead, only their spirit is alive. And I call them and ask them to surround my body. I think they are part of the orgone energy Wilhelm Reich discovered. And I call other people as well, mostly artists I met when I was young. Robert Filliou, David Zack, Sari Dienes, Ray Johnson, Jack Smith, Andy Warhol, Joseph Beuys, Cassandra von Rinteln and many others. I ask them to protect me from gentrification and don't let me become a Shinyist clone.

Well, I just bought a new iMac. One of the leading products of the current Shinyist technology. It completely seduced me and now it's hypnotizing me in my office. As I told you at the beginning I'm frightened and I'm ashamed of myself for being frightened. I'm afraid of becoming what I have never wanted to become. And that's why I am frightened when I'm staring at the shiny screen.

First performed at the Theater Center in march/2008 as part of Free Fall, a festival of new theater and performance art, presented in partnership with Harbourfront Centre's World Stage 08.

Photo documentation of Transmission Machine by Dean Goodwin, March/2008

Performance at Neutral Ground, Regina, Nov/2005

GOSPEL—SILENT MOVIE

She works in the streets of Tetropolis a brutal police state
Her partner is a drug dealer and gets killed during a police raid
Mary Magdalene arrives home to find him crucified on the wall
As she prays and mourns him he comes alive
His body is glowing like bright light
She wants to hug him but then he suddenly disappears
Mary Magdalene collapses in epileptic seizure
When she awakens she realizes that she is a virgin again
She cant believe in her fingers
She is terrified and enchanted at the same time
She realizes that it's time for a change to start a new life
She goes in exile and lives a solitary life in an abandoned building
She reads books writes poetry makes drawings practices yoga

***

A fugitive arrives from the failed Tetropolis revolution
Looking for hiding place and they meet
Mary Magdalene has a crash on him and hugs him with passion
As they make love the police arrive to arrest the fugitive
They rape and torture Mary Magdalene in front of him
They beat him up and take him to prison
Mary Magdalene collapses in epileptic seizure
Her bleeding body is glowing in the ruins
She miraculously gets healed
She realizes that she is a virgin again
She is shocked and delighted, she touches herself again and again
She has a new vision that she must return to Tetropolis

***

She joins a group of political activists
By chance she meets the fugitive,
S/he is now a transgender performer
Mary Magdalene learns that s/he was tortured and castrated in prison
They fall in love again
Mary Magdalene gives birth to a child
The police raids their home looking for evidences of conspiracy
They arrest both of them for subversive activities
They take them to prison
They fail to see the sleeping child covered with blankets

***

Mary Magdalene gets raped again by the prison guards
She collapses in epileptic seizure and this time she dies
The coroner tells to the guards that MM was a virgin
The guards laugh their heads off
The news of her death gets to the desperate fugitive
He hangs himself in his prison cell
The child is alone and crying

NEW YORK HEADQUARTERS OF NEOISM

MONTY CANTSIN

NEOISM NOW

DEAR

MONTY CANTSIN

This is to announce that the NEW YORK HEADQUARTERS
OF NEOISM is now open and starts its activities with a
street publicity campaign (glue and spray paint power).
Our office is in a secret place, hidden in obscurity, in
a fucked up and dirty recording studio decorated with a
red cross and the left overs of a dead rock'n'roll band.
Our few conspirators are in bad condition but ready for
action.

We are fed up with the disco-politics of business-art
galleries and clubs. East Village=Soho= $
A new revolution is up to date.

You can join us by calling yourself MONTY CANTSIN and by
doing everything in the name of NEOISM. This will create
confusion and make control impossible.

Do not call, write or try to contact us for more information.
You are in charge of everything.

YOUR IMMORTAL FRIEND

NEOISM NOW

MONTY CANTSIN

dance to the beat of neoism , dance the monty cantsin

Neoist Flyer, 1982

IT'S GONNA RAIN
FOR BROTHER WALTER VIA STEVE REICH

Communication is a big business you know and the news is the best selling merchandise. The Empire controls the means of information and nobody can fuck with the system. Imagine someone who wants to give a message that would change the world, an unknown prophet who spends many years, struggling to be heard:

> **I'm trying to make people listen.**
> **I'm trying to make people understand.**
> **I'm trying to make people believe.**
> **It's gonna rain, it's gonna rain, it's gonna rain!**

Nobody cares but a miracle happens and the world's biggest network suddenly decides to give this prophet a chance in a talk-show broadcast live all around the world. They create a huge publicity campaign unprecedented and hysterical, people are eagerly waiting to hear the Unknown Prophet and receive the message:

> **I'm trying to make people listen.**
> **I'm trying to make people understand.**
> **I'm trying to make people believe.**
> **It's gonna rain, it's gonna rain, it's gonna rain!**

The day comes, the world is in ecstasy and panic and everyone sits in front of their TV. The host of the program gives an introduction, the world becomes silent nobody moves. Nobody is born, nobody dies, this is a moment that never comes back. The Unknown Prophet takes a deep breath and begins to speak without delay:

> **I'm trying to make people listen.**
> **I'm trying to make people understand.**
> **I'm trying to make people believe.**
> **It's gonna rain, it's gonna rain, it's gonna rain!**

The world is astonished. What a joke. They were expecting something else, perhaps another more important message something that would scare them to death. The Unknown Prophet repeats it again. Nobody heard such a strange voice before screaming, trembling, praying and shouting, one has the feeling it isn't real:

I'm trying to make people listen.
I'm trying to make people understand.
I'm trying to make people believe.
It's gonna rain, it's gonna rain, it's gonna rain!

Some restless people finally break the silence and more and more join them with increasing anger, until it erupts like an unstoppable fire, the spectators feel they were betrayed. While people are storming the television stations, the producers are trying to save their lives, the army moves in to arrest the Prophet for generating chaos, confusion and disorder.

I'm trying to make people listen.
I'm trying to make people understand.
I'm trying to make people believe.
It's gonna rain, it's gonna rain, it's gonna rain!

Within a few minutes an emergency committee sentences the Unknown Prophet to death. The Unknown Prophet is taken and crucified and dies on the cross as it expected. Moments later it begins to rain, the heavy rain doesn't stop for 40 days, the disastrous flood kills everyone. Nobody escapes, nobody survives.

I'm trying to make people listen.
I'm trying to make people understand.
I'm trying to make people believe.
It's gonna rain, it's gonna rain, it's gonna rain!

The voice of Brother Walter, a Pentecostal street preacher, was the inspirational source and subject of Steve Reich's ground breaking loop composition It's gonna rain. Reich recorded Brother Walter's voice on a Sunday afternoon at Union Square in downtown San Francisco, sometime in jan/1965. Inspired by Reich's loop I "recreated" Brother Walter's speech in the late 80s while living in New York's Lower East Side and performing in the streets backed up by a ghetto blaster.

FILE CABINET MACHINERY

I admit I want to die of information overdozzzzzz

I get excited about managing information all the time. It would be even nicer to have a little more. To go over the flow. I was never paid a salary to keep things organized in my office. I do it for the sake of doing it. It's always crazy here but I learned to keep things moving and in tip-top shape. If things were quiet I would stir things up because total chaos is my home. That's what subversive elements have always done—they use telephones, megaphones, microphones, vocal cords, samplers, pirate transmitters, telepathic communication and computers to manipulate information, to stir things up and to put things back into disorder.

I have always worked at home full time, day and night. I always enjoyed the messes I'd made at home. And I could get a lot more done by extending my office into my bedroom. And I was the first to get a laptop because I needed more time to work on my ideas and commuting was the only time I had for extension. But I never carried a cell phone on the road because I prefer extrasensorial organs. I rather use telepathy to keep in touch with my conspirators and family. I also pray for help to my dead parents when I'm in the shower. I often initiate crises when I'm on the road. I know this goes against the grain. I receive tons of exciting messages and I answer all the psychotronic calls in order to keep the conspiracy going. I use a coat hanger antenna attached to my head to increase the power of my brain waves. Meanwhile I listen to music, make drawings, read several zines and books at once and plunder ideas for The Book of Neoism.

The other day I realized how happy I am of managing information. I feel like a damned terrorist or a utopian revolutionary. Most of my waking hours are spent opening and closing file cabinets, pulling the drawers in and out, making noise by banging the metal hardware of the cabinets, and thinking about all the other people doing the same thing. It's a worldwide performance, group sex. My life couldn't be more creative. I love to fuck file cabinets! Fucked by file cabinets!

I'm making the messes—interesting, vital messes. Hardware and software are interconnected. I find I'm an extension of all softwares and I am extended by softwares. I want to use the most powerful software as a template for my totalitarian, subversive behaviour.

Without technology I'm confused, suicidal, and lost. There are loose-ends, but these loose-ends dangle in the never-never land beyond the control of the system, the network … somewhere beyond my office. I think about these loose ends when I'm exercising, inhaling and exhaling or playing with my children in the nearby park.

Long live inanity

Long live inanity, oh yeah. I'm being buried with mind-blowing Neoist trash. And I love it! Totally (un)(ultra)realistic techno-trash trance-generated for over-stimulation, by my co-conspirators going through the pelvic (pro)motions. They are convinced that they're being ultimately subversive by issuing anti-establishment personal statements on absolutely everything, like for example their increased number of techno-tantric neo-orgasmic pleasure per day through 100% vegan post-trans-anal extra-vitro-alien hyper-manipulations, and they're totally certain that they can change the world, because they're having interactive ecstasy when they simply spread their legs far and wide in front of their designer work station surrounded by acoustical panel system, additional information storage furniture and contemporary style executive steelcase file cabinets. (I love these cabinets!)

Those who use their wet tongue might be forgotten. And even those who hold their orgasm for the longest duration will not always be remembered. But people who choose their cyber-positions wisely will be kept alive by the indiscreet co-conspirators, those with ultra-radical multi-orgasmic-identities maintained by dot-cuming continuously on absolutely everything. They issue high volumes of infrared-tetra-electro-cum in order to assert, and maintain huge pseudo-hardons for their very digital existence.

These intersex-maniac desktop beat-cons of mega-giga-personality are simply filling the dotcom-scum vacuum. Enduring long, socially bankrupt hours at their 'work-stations,' they enjoy a surplus of privacy in their respective remote locations, but feel a definite need to participate in a kind of simulated office orgy. In this way blacklistservers licking communities-of-interest simulate highrise office sex, where co-conspirators actually rub their skin, smoke pot and drink coolers while simultaneously fucking file cabinets and really keeping in touch through e-communication. Remotely · networked co-conspirators also crave day-to-day contact with each other. In the absence of daily physical contact, this simulated office encounter quickly revs up and becomes the surrogate display of the group's cohabitation on a specific network or blacklist. Intercourse-nets provide the breeding ground for insider-attitudes, thus promoting the formulation of semi-coherent erotic submission directives.

There is another side to this simulated, surrogate-office-orgy scenario. Many of the most energetic, totally obsessive sex-transmitters garner energy from their frustration with the banality of their screen-based 'blow jobs.' Their outreach is driven by a positive desire: a craving for real flesh.

These individuals, if they make their living shackled to a keyboard and computer screen, find themselves perpetually on-line, and available for virtual intercourse with absolutely everybody. Dominators, pornographers, adult-writers, genital terrorists, gender mongers, cyber-hedonists, office fetishists, s/m-animators, etc., etc., many of them self-employed and telecommuting, find their loneliness more tolerable if they are reaching out and making direct contact with others in domains supplementary to their compensatory labour.

These peripheral, diversionary exchanges perforate and are feathered into normal workday fucking. Fortunately interpersonal technorgasmic communication is often systematically pursued and practiced like subvertising other forms of phallic, pussy influence. The last orgasm is never the last orgasm. But like an unsuccessful attempt to add an inch, the transmission process often amounts to nothing more than a persistent, relentless manifestation of cybersportfucking, mere proof of softwarepleasure, a vaguely self-affirming pelvic stroke machinery bang-bang, a bare-bones signifier of robotic ecstasy ... A techno-porn of collective S.O.S., a cyber-bureaunoid furniture-sex Payday extravaganza ...!

Fresh faces

For the past thousand years I've been in communication with millions of Neoists through the decentralized conspiracy networks via hyper-terrestrial telepathy and extrasensorial voice-link. It has been interesting to supplement our para-normal wire coat hanger links with ultra-psychotronic pseudo-pictures and more expensive chemo-hallucinatory inner-voice sub-conversations. We still keep things tied together with sex, drugs, and rock'n'roll. Ecstatic hallucinations still rule in terms of stimulating exchanges and getting things done. Powder talks are very useful in terms of reports and planning. Conference calls make a lot more sense with hyper-chemical support. I've really enjoyed getting a broader sense of my co-workers, the way they look and talk when they are loaded with drugs and alcohol while listening to trance-techno beat.

I've also noticed a lot of horny, extra-orgasmic humour that seems to be generated by these turbo-hallucinatory alien encounters. In a situation where a bunch of us get together on a shared bill to get high, it's crazy the way everything is put forth with obvious neo-erotic gestures and extra-promising smiles, no matter how boring the party's underground guest DJ is. There seems to be an unwritten code of behaviour that forces everyone to be overtly sexy and predisposed to techno-noise belly-dance at the expense of total communication and industrial culture. This go-physical code of conduct is particularly glaring to those jerking off in these meetings off-camera and sober.

Our corporation has a trans-para-emergency policy. The party times, drug dealers' addresses and sex workers' haciendas are published in advance on the corporation's employees' home page. Everyone in the corporation is welcome to get high on every possible drug, should the agenda be of interest, or if they want to get a sense of what it would be like to have fun with particular individuals at a later date.

Personally I find the time just before and after these webcam orgies to be the most revealing moments in the life of the corporation. If you look at the daily meeting schedule and log on ten or fifteen minutes before a meeting commences, you will find that some of the participants jerk off early. They are usually sitting there in their cubicles dealing with on-screen porn or attending to their intimate e-mail or phone-sex conversations. It always strikes me how dead their faces look before the drugs kick in and they put on their Neoist open-pop-star personalities. It's the same after a meeting when they're jerking off alone again.

If people would masturbate carefully in front of their video mirrors, they would notice a certain deadness in their faces. People sitting at computers watching porn sites for long hours have this extra gravity in their expressions, especially in the muscles around their mouths. When I look in on people getting ready for a hit, or just after, it is striking how they appear emotionally mute. This vacant, drained appearance triggers my own depressing introspection. I've become aware of my own depression through the numbing fatigue around my mouth, the way my face looks and feels heavy when I have that sinking feeling of desire for a long vacation in the mountains or at the ocean.

This is what I've learned from working in an organization linked by webcam dealers. I've learned that we're not networking on a high-tech level of sexual repression. I don't really believe the file cabinet machines and information storage furniture are draining us, but there is something desperate about the orgasmic explosions that erupt in the office when we're interacting on camera. When I feel numb and emotionally exhausted, and look particularly drained around my mouth, I usually try to go outside for a walk, to look at some fresh faces. Or at the very least I go and climb up a tree. I find it helps to go outside, or at least to go someplace else where I'm not constantly urged to blow my mind and fuck my brains out.

THE SECOND 6 FINGER PLAN
0101 1985 ..... — .. .1231.1990

THE SECOND SIX FINGER PLAN

proposed by MONTY CANTSIN

The concept of AKADEMGOROD was initiated by Napoleon
Moffat in New York,on march 18,1982, during APT 5
(Fifth International Apartment Festival).

"Neoists should be in search for the city of
scientists, should be in search for AKADEMGOROD...
The goals of the crusade are to find the city and
then, establish the reality of NEOISM into the
reality of AKADEMGOROD....."

-The Legitimacy of Akademgorod
by Napoleon Moffat

It was collectively adopted and developped into
the idea of NEOIST PROMISED LAND.
Architectonic plans were begun by Boris Wanowitch
in 1983.
"A TRIP TO AKADEMGOROD" test-book was published
by Vittore Baroni of AGENZIA NEOISTA,Italy in early
1984.
In the same year the International Neoist Network
was re-created and changed to AKAUCN - Akademgorod
United Cells Of Neoism.
AKA-Cards (AKAUCN Citizen Cards) are distributed
by Neoist Embassy,Montreal and Neoist DATA Cell,
Dysart,Scotland.
....
"Neoism has always been and always will be" I say,
however operations of Neoist Conspiracy were only
initiated in 1979, in Montreal.
Here is a short summary of the FIRST FIVE YEARS of
Neoist Activity (1979-1984):

A:the formation of an international research network
B:the development of APT FESTevents
C:the inauguration of AKA PLAN (Akademgorod)
D:the search for the Unknown Neoist
E:the fight for total freedom through dance/music

The Neoist Network's First European Training Camp was
held in Wurzburg, West-Germany, in june, 1982.
This event continued with "Balkanska Kampanja" sept,1982.

NEOISM NEOISM AKAUCN
AKADEMGOROD UNITED CELLS OF NEOISM
NEOISM cell cell

NEOISM

THE SECOND 6 FINGER PLAN
0101 1985 ----- 1231 1990

After this short history lesson let me to introduce
you to our next project and give a fast-food descrip
tion-clip of "THE SECOND SIX FINGER PLAN" 1985-1990.

During the next six years we have to find Akademgorod,
the Promised Land of Neoism. We dont know where and
how but we have to work out a strategy.

1985 is the year of individual proposals to improve
the plan. Several meetings and APT Fests are going
to take place in North America and Europe. A book
about the final plan and strategy will be published
at the end of nov., and sent it to all network members,
sympathizers and the media. Rainy days.

1986 is the year of financial operations.
At the end of this year the first one million $
will be deposited into Akademgorod's bank account.
There will be an APT Fest in Tokyo. Hot summer.

1987 is the year of the place. It must be found,
taken over or bought. Construction begins. Lot of
jobs. Wind.

1988 is the year of construction. Messages from
several planets. F.A.B.'s world tour. Storms. Fire.

1989 is the second year of construction.
Inauguration of the Swimming Pool of Immortality.
Waves.

1990 is the year of final touches.
Inauguration of AKADEMGOROD PROMISED LAND OF
NEOISM, at New Year's Eve Chapati Ball. Bright blue
sky. Lot of stars.

You can say it could not be done. We wont listen.
We are at the beginning of an unprecedented history.

Kill normality before it kills you.

Your immortal friend

Monty Cantsin

AMBASSADE NEOISTE / NEOIST EMBASSY
1020 Lajoie ave. Outremont, Que.
H2V 1N4 Canada   tel. (514) 273-3901

THE SECOND 6 FINGER PLAN
0101 1985 ---- 1231 1990

SCRIPTURE

SKETCH FOR A GUERRILLA VIDEO STAGED IN THE RUINS AT A DEMOLITION/CONSTRUCTION SITE

In a hidden corner of devastation, piles of leftover cocaine and barrels of cherry flavored cyanide are the remainders of a final doomsday. Indestructible *humanoid scibot slaves* are the only survivors in the ruins. Their sensory system and modus operandi are equally damaged. Their hybrid characters are inspired by mythology, science fiction and history. They collect detritus and impatiently reprocess information found in movies, books, art and revolutionary propaganda. Two of these damaged, out of order *biobots* meet in a deadzone of ruins. Their challenging behavior gets exposed through disabled verbal communication and mimicking gestures.

***

A blind and mute, disabled scibot, *The Veteran*, emerges at the campsite of a narcissistic creature possessing prophetic powers. *Neo-Narcissus* (*NN*) is looking at her reflection in a pond. She throws a rock at it. *The Veteran* is walking alone, stops, looks, touches, picks up things from the ground. The water gets motionless again and *NN* observes *The Veteran's* face behind her own reflection. *NN* turns to *The Veteran*. He is blindfolded and carries a large black hockey bag on his back. *The Veteran* tries to express himself in words but in vain.

***

They walk to *NN's* camp. *The Veteran* empties his bag on the ground in the middle of *NN's* living space. Books, video tapes and other obsolete material fall to the grand. He pulls out a piece of paper from among the things. "*I AM THE REVOLUTION*" is written on it.

***

NN and *The Veteran* are creating a ritual with objects, gestures, fire, smoke. She tells *The Veteran* that the only way for him to accomplish his mission and start a revolution is to die first. Then his spirit will succeed.

"YOU MUST DIE IF YOU WANT TO SUCCEED. ONLY YOUR SPIRIT CAN CARRY THE WEIGHT OF REVOLUTION."

She tells him.

The Veteran agrees.

***

NN fucks *The Veteran* to death. *The Veteran* shoots blood like fluid from his mouth into *NN's* body as he dies from a deadly orgasm. *NN* puts his body in his black hockey bag, sets it on fire and kicks it into the pond.

***

The day after, while *NN* washes her underwear, suddenly the reflection of *The Veteran* appears in the water.

WARNING WARNING WARNING WARNING AVERTISSEMENT AVERTISSEMENT AVERTISSEMENT WARNING
AVERTISSEMENT WARNING AVERTISSEMENT WARNING AVERTISSEMENT WARNING AVERTISSEMENT WARN
WARNING AVERTISSEMENT WARNING AVERTISSEMENT WARNING AVERTISSEMENT WARNING AVERTISSEM
WARNING WARNING AVERTISSEMENT AVERTISSEMENT WARNING WARNING AVERTISSEMENT WARNING

the extraterrestrial neoists,temporarly staying on the earth,call for all the in-
habitants of the planet:
"terminate every relationship with the state powers,the church and all social,poli
tical and cultural organizations.
resign your nationalities to get away from formal obligations.
leave the offices and factories.
open the borders and give up the zone-mode of life.
not accept any allotments -money or other gifts- in exchange for your freedom.
paralyse the police and army which are your paralysers.
this is the only possibility of obtaining the cosmic-free-way of your souls.
this is the only way to get the earth into the membership of "free planets galaxy".
do this,and your physical existence will not be determined by the lies of science.
death is not true.
enter into the eternity."
. . . .

les extraterrestres néoistes,demeurant temporairement sur la terre,lancent un
appel à tous les habitants de la planète:
"cessez toute relation avec les puissances de l'etat,l'eglise et toutes les
organisations sociales,politiques et culturelles.
renoncez à votre nationalité afin d'éviter tout devoir dicté par les conventions.
quittez les bureaux et les usines.
ouvrez les frontières et abandonnez cette manière bornée de vivre.
n'acceptez aucune rémunération -en argent ou en espèces- en échange de votre
liberté.
paralysez la police et l'armée qui vous paralysent.
ceci est la seule perspective en vue d'arriver à la libre avenue cosmique de
vos âmes.
ceci est la seule façon d'attirer la terre à adhérer à la "galaxie des planètes
libres".
faites ceci,et votre existence physique ne sera plus déterminée par les mensonges
de la science.
la mort n'est pas vraie.
entrez dans l'éternité."

ANNO NEOISTO PRIMERO
PLANETO

Neoist Warning, Montreal, 1979

UFO

IT WAS VERY NICE
IT WAS VERY NICE IT WAS VERY VERY
VERY NICE IT WAS VERY VERY VERY VERY VERY VERY VERY NICE
IT WAS VERY VERY VERY VERY VERY VERY VERY NICE NICE NICE NICE NICE NICE
NICE NICE NICE IT WAS VERY NICE VERY NICE VERY NICE VERY NICE IT WAS VERY
NICE TO SEE YOU SEE YOU SEE YOU SEE YOU SEE YOU SEE YOU SEE YOU AND TALK
TALK TALK TALK TALK TALK TALK TALK TALK TALK TALK TALK TALK TALK TALK TALK TALK
TALK TALK TALK TALK TALK TALK TALK TALK TALK TALK TALK TALK TALK TALK TALK
TALK TALK TALK TALK TALK TALK ABOUT TALK ABOUT TALK ABOUT TALK ABOUT
TALK ABOUT TALK ABOUT IT WAS VERY NICE IT WAS VERY NICE IT WAS VERY NICE
IT WAS VERY NICE TO SEE YOU SEE YOU SEE YOU SEE YOU
IT WAS VERY NICE TO SEE YOU
AND TALK ABOUT
REVOLUTION

IAMMONTYCANTSIN, band portrait by Ariane Laezza, may 18/2017, Toronto. From left to right: Monty Cantsin electro-drums/garbage-can, Monty Cantsin vocals, Monty Cantsin scrapmetal-noise/electro-beat, Monty Cantsin flag waving, Monty Cantsin vocals/ loopmachine, Monty Cantsin, vocals

SOUNDS LIKE NEOISM?!

Falseintro

Was Akademgorod-Atlantis the landing base for the Neoist UFOnauts who came to Earth millions of years ago? This question is only a semi-silly poetical impulse for the reader's mind and hardly has anything to do with the subject. Neoism?! is a put on. There is no such thing as Neoism?!. Neoism?! is what makes Neoism?! obsolete. Failure is the armature of Neoism?!. The theory of Neoism?! encourages anyone to do anything in the name of Neoism?!. And some people are desperately trying to (ab)use this term to define themselves and their doings. I am one of the promoters of abusement (twin sisterbrother of irritainment and vextasy). But what can you define with a term that has no definition? That's exactly what we are interested in: to define by undefining. We are determined to confuse. I don't intend to spend much time here to undefine Neoism?!. I have done that at many occasions and in different forms. This short introduction to Neoism?! is only to serve one purpose: to create the illusion that I know what I'm talking about. The real subject of this text is my experimentations with sounds (like Neoism?!, of course).

Undisciplined crap

I've said on many occasions that I only do what I like to do. Consequently, someone can conclude what my determination suggests: I must be satisfied with what I have accomplished. Wrong. I'm never satisfied with what I have done. Because even if you only do what you like to do the results are not necessarily what you expect. After finishing a new piece, for example, my immediate reaction is that I hate it all. And almost instantly I start working on a different version of the same thing, using the most extremist methods of decomposition, to destroy, to annihilate my original idea (metamorphoses of the Shiva cycle of construction-deconstruction-reconstruction). And when this has been done I feel much better. The closer I get to my own work the more I hate it. So I try to distance myself from what I have accomplished. This symptom must be the result of the fact that since I only do what I like to do, I always tend to overdo things, to put too much effort in one single idea. I would like to be able to produce some sort of random noise that can only be summed up as undisciplined crap. That would be perhaps my greatest achievement. I want to reach this simplicity to make sure that I've got away from all formalities of composition. But unfortunately my undeniably intellectual character always makes my work too sophisticated and adventurous. I have to fight with physical and psychological factors to overcome on my needs and reduce activity fields to a minimum. I want to do things without any attachment to memory and without any reference to history. And this can not be done without sweat, blood, pain, abandonment and self-destruction.

Scrapmetal stimuli

Performance always has been more important for me than anything else and performance means body and hardware. It is great to be able to create noise through scientific methods and I'm still under the spell of Nicola Tesla's old concept of mechanical resonance created with a tiny oscillator that could split the Earth in two. It is very flattering to know that you can destroy the whole world by simply pushing a button. I will never deny it, but I also like to sweat and bleed when I perform. I like to use scrapmetal, junk, anything that can make noise and I can afford. With an oil drum and a couple of metal sticks you can produce a variety of sounds, but there is much more in scrapmetal performance than just banging on the surface of objects or trying to do what you can do with a traditional drum kit. To explore the sound of an object you have to find the right technique that will do it. Beating the shit out of a garbage can will create a very powerful sound. But there are many other methods as well and you develop them by practicing.

I got my first lessons by watching DJ Steve playing at the Rivington School Garden, in the Lower East Side of Manhattan. He was able to produce amazingly surprising, unheard sounds with his _oil drum/corrugated metal sheet/threaded rod kit_. He used the rod on the corrugated sheet as a contrabassist does it with a bow, with his other hand rhythmically jerking the corrugated sheet on the top of the oil drum. The physical aspects of a performance are principal factors. I like to use my body and get in close physical relations with objects, machines and people. Seems like a macho attitude, but I'm not trying to express my maleness or show my ability to be a strong man. For me performance is a matter of stimuli. Emotions also can play some role in it especially when some uncooperating organizers provoke my temper. My reason for doing a few hundred push-ups every day is not so much to increase my chest muscles, but rather to generate enough chemical substances (endorphins) to stimulate my mind and body mechanism.

I agree with Stelarc that the body is obsolete. It has always been. I like the idea of robot-expansions, and it is very realistic today to perfect, to expand, or to remake our body parts with the use of technology and to increase the physical aspects of performance. What I hate is the frustrating fact that high technology means high expenses and usually I can afford only junkyard prices. I don't care about what the audience wants to hear or see. I care about more what they don't. I do everything according to my intentions and instincts. I always plan some of it beforehand, but the moment I start a performance I know that I wont follow my original ideas. I never do. When I can afford it I work with collaborators and we all do our own thing without much instructions. Everything sounds much better when things happen spontaneously. When you have pre-set musical ambitions and admiration for musicians, recording studios and the audience, then your work won't be strong enough to distinguish it from mainstream products. In my sets the audience only hear the sound of scrap and ugly machines and see some people trying to dismantle the stage. The noise I produce often empties the place, or under better circumstances, the performance ends in a riot.

Armature/Accumulations

My office is located on Richmond Street West, Toronto. Right now I'm sitting in front of my computer and I'm writing this monologue of Istvan Kantor that at first was supposed to be an interview with (a) Monty Cantsin. I'm trying to re-decompose this piece for the fourth time. I am listed at the lobby as PUPPET GOVERNMENT. This is my business executive office. "It looks like a junk-shop," visitors usually say. Among the second-hand goods and industrial hardware I have accumulated here during the past recent years are a dozen file cabinets, hundreds of broken irons, AC/DC motors, metal rods, chains, kitchen appliances, barbed wire, old loudspeakers, blades, broken TVs, plastic screens for video projection, metal garbage cans, meatgrinders, corrugated metal sheets, all kind of cables, a big collection of coat-hangers, a few thousand uncut keys, a tin coffin, bedsprings, etc. And I also stock my kinetic armature and furniture. A hydraulic robot platform, a couple of kinetic file cabinets, barbed wire blade percussions, rotating office chairs, shaking tables, etc., they were all made to make noise.

Another object that takes up quite a big space here is a rather conceptual silent sound-piece called "*Overprepared broken vibraphone waiting for takeoff.*" It incorporates the parts of an old vibraphone, three meat grinders and nine electric irons. In one side of the room I keep my more advanced technology of video/audio equipment. I use digital samplers to accumulate sounds and to make multiple loops of many layers, for example. Accumulation is the key word not only for my sound-making methods but for my life in general. I accumulate debts, unpaid bills, anger, futile plans, hungry children … Years before, when I felt I wanted to change name, I just threw away the old one. Now I accumulate them, thus presently my full name is (Istvan Kantor) Monty Cantsin? AMEN!

Delayed acoustics

My work often gets criticized as sensationalist, and sensationalism, they say, is a cheap motive. I like cheap motives. I don't get offended by damning critical judgements, rather enjoy them. I'm highly self-critical. Insults are important strategical linguistic devices of Neoism?!. First of all, it is not easy to create sensations and it will be more and more difficult in the future since we have witnessed too many. It needs a great and somehow sophisticated input to trigger a reaction. When you splash blood on the wall of a museum you generate lots of noise. There is a sensationalist aspect in it. The making of blood-X is a very particular ambient noise performance that gets amplified by the delayed acoustics of the media. In fact, you can only be sensationalistic if you get amplified by the media. Otherwise nobody will know about what you have done since you have done it in almost total secrecy and silence. And it also happens that museums suppress media information by their corrupt means of friendly relationships with news editors. They don't want the publicity because it wouldn't look good on them and would bring up too many questions about the function of such institutions.

Contrarily to the surprise attack of blood action, the megaphone performance is usually publicized and presented under normal staged circumstances. And these normal circumstances are rather depressing because nobody cares about this type of noise stuff that is still considered too weird and inaccessible. The noise of blood actions might be analogue with my megaphonic convulsions, but while the blood performances create lots of media reaction, enlarging the fields of communication, my megaphone concerts shape a different figure of the unknown invisible underground experimentalist.

(F)unmusical terms

Noise is pure and simple consciousness. Tonalitism is totalitarianism. The world is audible. Silence is nonsense. In 1947, in his address to a conference of leading musicians, Andrei A. Zhdanov, member of the Central Committee of the Communist Party, stated that music must be tranquil, reassuring, and calm. And he added: "Your task is to prove the superiority of Soviet music, to create great Soviet music." If muzak (tranquil, reassuring and calm) is THE great Soviet music then what is noizak? Zhdanov's answer: "The infiltrating element of subversion, the sound of the abnormal!" I always keep searching for new terms for my dictionary of linguistic devices. Noizak is perhaps one of them. I'm using it occasionally, but without any serious effort. I guess it was just an immediate and obvious reflex reaction to muzak when I first heard it. There is nothing much to explain about it unless one never heard of muzak. But then again why one would want to learn about noizak who doesn't know about muzak? Why not? My children know everything about noizak but never heard of muzak (our family life is a noise friendly production). Another one is nichtmusik, German for no-music. No-music is too used, nichtmusik seems to have more irony because of its assonance with nachtmusik which means a pleasant romantic night concert. The best term that includes the necessary irony and the double negation of serious music is (f)unmusical. Be (f)unmusical!

I'm sure that this time even tENTATIVELY, a cONVENIENCE agrees with me. (We have had various disagreements and personality clashes during the past two decades.) He also likes to use his own terms and proposes a few of them to describe sound related activities. From among them I mention usic, booed usic, and the more recent low classical usic. Usic intend to emphasize the fact that sounds can be used without musical intent. Booed usic, my favourite term, includes the audience's reaction as a determining factor of usic events. Low Classical Usic is a somewhat more complex semi-socio-political term to which tENT sacrificed an eight-page yet unpublished essay. The best new terms are those already existing words in which you only have to change a single letter to create a new meaning. This new meaning will also include the old one because that's what the new word will always remind you of. That's why Neoism?! incorporates all the previous isms. It would be a good idea to put together a (f)unmusical (sic)tionary.

Syphon story

I have been always doing many things at once, from a very early age, poetry, music, fiction, theater, graphic art, film, video, whatever. I have never been able to concentrate on one single thing and stop dissipating my energies. Being squandered is my favourite way of existence.

While my father worried about me dissipating my energies, wasting my time and squandering my talents, for me dissipating my energies was the greatest virtue, wasting my time was a redeeming philosophy, and squandering my talents was a way of creative living I planned for my whole life.

And as you keep doing things each discipline challenges you with more and different possibilities. I've been working with noise for a long time; however, because of the everchanging creative conditions, at certain periods this work has been overshadowed by other involvements. I was in my early teens when rock music became a world wide form of youth revolt and a multi-billion business of industrial entertainment. I have played in many bands and I have written hundreds of songs. But, at the same time, I was also involved with unpopular forms like anti-music, spontaneous improvisation, noise.

One early example of this is the syphon-music concept, a neo-dada experience originated in the late 60s, early 70s in Budapest. The basic idea was to provoke the audience through the unskilled use of musical instruments. You could only be a participant of a syphon-music performance if you couldn't play any instruments, or, if you happened to know how to play piano, for example, then you had to play trumpet or violin. But at each occasion you had to change instrument to make sure that you wouldn't get familiar with any of them. Besides using classical instruments, from cello to clarinet via piano, and producing orchestral confusion at exhibition openings or parties, we also passed ourselves for rock bands. Our method was to go to a club, introduce ourselves to the organizers as a new band and ask them to let us play during the intermission. Since we didn't ask for money and we knew how to talk them into it, they usually agreed. When we were up on stage we immediately untuned the instruments and produced some kind of irritating noise. It usually took a few minutes until the organizers got over their stupefaction and tried to pull us off the stage, resulting in even more chaos. We became infamous and got banned from many clubs. But eventually, after repeating this prank a number of times, the rumours made us known in the music circuits and we got invited to do our own shows. This kind of success reversed the original idea and turned it into an accepted form of entertainment, and, of course, these consequences meant the end of the syphon-music era.

A few years later, in 1978, while developing the open-pop-star idea with David Zack in Portland, Oregon, I practiced spontaneous improvisation with the Smegmas. Members of the group lived together in a commune and played every night in the basement studio of the Smegma house. Though they released many records and occasionally performed at local venues as well as elsewhere on the west coast, they remained in passionate obscurity. David and I, later joined by Ju Suk Reet Meat from Smegma, formed a new performance group, The Monty Cantsin Ism b. band. To describe our free style I reapplied the syphon-music concept. Of course it was a different version, taking inspiration from many different sources including mail-art, fluxus, punk, Hungarian folk, concrete poetry, etc., producing a hybrid sound, somewhere between street blues and avant-garde music. We provoked or irritated the audience with surprising and sometimes silly sound elements such as collective breathing, typing, blowing up paper bags on each other's heads, reading from a music dictionary, etc.

At the same time I also performed different solo acts under different names. I played detuned guitar, resonating the strings with the use of electric tools, under the alias of Bertolt Bartok punk-folk singer, or recited hymnic found poetry to the sound of an electric shaver in the name of Monty Cantsin. I released a record with some of the Monty Cantsin Ism b. band stuff in a limited edition of 200, in 1978. Some of my Smegma collaborations are also on records that are probably impossible to find today.

Street performance by Monty Cantsin, NYC, Lower East Side, 1986

Megaphonic convulsions

Megaphony is a term I've used for a number of years (since 1989) to describe my works in which I use the portable megaphone as the main source of sound. By blowing, licking or sucking the megaphone's mouth piece (the lung/mouth human system can be replaced by air compressor/rubber pipe mechanism), the megaphone functions as an airophone instrument, made from a microphone, amp and speaker. With the use of the megaphone, a primitive noise making device, I'm able to create yet unheard, powerful as well as irritating, vextatic (vexation + ecstasy) sounds, somewhere between animal screaming and alien vocal signals, farting and explosion, sounds that are mentally and physically difficult to endure. In the creation of megaphonic noise both physical performance and technology (analog and digital) are equally important. I use samplers to capture and to accumulate the sound of the megaphone directly from a mic or through voice processors.

Through its absurd detournement the megaphone becomes an instrument of noise, a contemporary trumpet of doom. Because the megaphone is mostly used as a low tech tool by riot police, demonstrators or street speakers, its image and sound reflects the accuracy of social unrest, frustration and alert. I've used the megaphone as a usical instrument for almost a decade now and I've developed my standard improvisational techniques. I have made countless sound recordings and videos of megaphony, and, *The Anti-Cycles of Megaphony*, a work I devoted to the exploration of this particular instrument, is still a work in progress. *Escape From Freedom* (1991), *Jericho* (1991), *Barricades* (1992) are among the many videos that explore the megaphone and its sound with passionate determination to assault and to subvert.

From the megaphone performances I have done up to today I like to mention that of Mexico city (at X-Teresa), because that was the only time that my original and rather symbolical intention to break walls with the sound of the megaphone (trumpet of doom) became a realistic dangermotive, and according to my sound man, who was ordered by the organizers to keep the volume low and each time I signalled to increase it he pretended pushing it to the maximum, the organizers were worried that the already inclined old church would collapse due to the high frequency noise.

Frigophony monument

While having a conversation in the kitchen, we notice the noise of the refrigerator when it stops working, causing a sudden silence. This silence reveals a whole world of ambient sound that fills the rooms of our home.

I became interested in the refrigerator as object (only many years later as sound source) at around age 6 or 7 when I discovered an old appliance in the basement of our country house and used to hide things in it. This lifelong inspiration later continued with various installations and performances in which I placed objects inside refrigerators. "The frigidaire of Marcel Duchamp" (1985), an expanded video-performance and song (released by Maldoror records in 1987, NYC), marks the continuation of this special interest. I have exhibited my sticker collection on refrigerator doors throughout the 80s. I have made my first recordings of refrigerator noise (mostly for my own pleasure) in 1986, after the surprising result of an interview tape I recorded in the kitchen. Since then I have incorporated sampled refrigerator noise in sound works on several occasions.

Among the household sound devices perhaps the refrigerator is what can be found in any average home, mostly in the kitchen. And when I think about that a very large part of the world's population listens to this sound everyday, I still get fascinated. And I'm not the only one. tENTATIVELY, a cONVENIENCE's recent review, "Egnekn's fridge," in *Musicworks* No 63, is now an official document on the subject. He reviews a cassette of refrigerator noise, credited to a certain Egnekn (I won't disclose the origin of this obvious pseudoname). He also mentions another recording of the same type, "The Kenmore Symphony—in 2 movements" by Komar & Melamid. So we can say that the concrete noise of the refrigerator made its way into recording history. But would anyone listen to this sound if it wasn't built into this special kitchen appliance? Would you buy recordings of refrigerator noise? Years ago perhaps the answer would be a definite NO, but today it is not all that evident.

It would be very appropriate to pay tribute to the refrigerator, the world's greatest household "classical" drone instrument, icon of aural ambience and kitchen-noizak. Therefore I propose a project, intitled

FRIGOPHONY MONUMENT, that puts the refrigerator back into revolution. I also propose FRIGOPHONY to be used as a general term for the total world of ambient sound created by any home hardware like heating, air-conditioning, fluorescent lighting and cooking devices. The FRIGOPHONY MONUMENT consists of all the working refrigerators of the world forming a pseudo-monumentalist anti-sculpture. In this simple acoustic presentation the sound of the refrigerators are "amplified" by the global number of machines to dominate the world wide frigophonic sound manifesto. No computers, no digital equipment, not even a speaker (the refrigerators are the speakers) are needed.

Time has come to (re)discover the ambient sound devices of everyday life and enshrine the cultural values of the refrigerator. If this seemingly simple idea needs more justification, I can mention its many different borderline aspects (which might be boring and didactic), among them the boundaries of concrete-noise and psycho-acoustics, the inspiration of fluxus-events and situationism, the stimulating areas between poetry and performance. Frigophony questions the perception and capacity of hearing and investigates the relations between physics, bio-structure and psychology. Frigophony makes "the sound of the refrigerator" more interesting than the sound of the refrigerator.

Subway singer/beggar in Paris, 1976/77. Photo Zsuzsa Fehér.

The singer's cv

I'm basically a singer and I sometimes wonder why it takes so much trouble to keep being a singer. I grew up singing folk songs, pop songs, classical songs, revolutionary songs, communist workman songs. I sang in school choirs and listened to our eclectic record collection at home. I learned hundreds of songs by heart and entertained my family and friends. I started playing guitar and writing my own songs in my early teens. Soon I formed my first bands, but I also played solo. At around age19 I already gained a fair amount of popularity for writing rock-lyrics. I was also known as a solo performer, singing Bob Dylan style protest songs with guitar and harmonica. At the same time I experimented with avant-garde music as well. One of the consequences of this interest later has been the exploration of syphon-music (see Syphon story segment).

It was all very natural for me to try different directions and get involved with diverse styles and trends. I kept this attitude all my life and perhaps this unsteady, consistently inconsistent, nebulous nature led me to the open fields of Neoism?!. With my own group, known as Kantor Inform, I performed at festivals and special events all over the country, got recorded at the Hungarian Radio, but our experimental musical style, sometime labeled as new urban folk, added with politically critical inciting lyrics, made us part of the unofficial counter-culture. More and more we got isolated and ended up being an apartment group (that's how I came up with the apartment festival concept which I applied a few years later to develop Neoist events).

At this time of isolation and misery, in 1976, David Zack, American-Canadian mail-artist, writer, singer, cello and tenor guitar player, came to Budapest to have an exhibition at the Young Artists' Club. His extreme character impressed me a great deal and he gave me the necessary impulse I needed to change my life. Shortly after his visit I left the country. Couple of days before my departure we recorded most of our songs on a reel to reel tape recorder in the living room. I have this tape in my archive. For one year I was a street and subway singer/beggar in Paris. With two local musicians I also formed a new version of Kantor Inform and we played a few gigs in Paris, toured in the south of France and recorded a never published album for RTF

(French Radio/TV). I have this tape as well. In Paris I got inspiration from anarchists and punks.

My singing carrier continued to mutate in the next few years in Portland and in Montreal. I have already summed up my Portland experience under the above Syphon story segment. In Montreal I met Lion Lazer (now Zilon) with whom I practiced brain-music and bright-music. We came up with these terms to describe our improvisational, and more less ambient, style. Of course, in my archive I have a few reels of home made recordings of this period as well. Lazer was my partner in the launch of Neoism?! in Montreal, in 1979. We produced many "piano pieces" together in which the piano functioned more as a performance object than a musical instrument.

During one of these performances an almost fatal accident occurred. As I was pushing around an upright piano in a gallery while the naked Lazer was lying on the top of it, the piano became unbalanced and turned over. Lazer fell under the heavy instrument and was very lucky to only break one arm. Most of our experimentation with music of this period meant the same type of manifesto like simple actions or theatrical performances. These activities created scandals in the local art scene and turned us into infamous, subversive elements. Consequently we gained popularity in the new-wave, punk circles. I've always got more inspiration in night clubs than in galleries.

I kept enlarging my contacts through mail-art and through traveling as well. A series of international Neoist apartment festivals characterized my activities in the early 80s. These officially unofficial festivals meant lots of diverse experimentation including sound and music. The fertile ground of these wank fests helped me, and perhaps everyone else, to develop new concepts. tENTATIVELY's booed usic; Zack's unending voice/cello improvisations; Gordon W.'s tabla performances; Keane's lounge singing style; Zbigniew's minimalistic computer compositions; Bonbon's monotone sequencer pulsations; Lazer's ambient synt sounds; Kent Tate's piano pieces; Moondog's rock singing; Alan Lord's guitar pieces. These are only some examples.

Later, in 1985, I published a limited edition of music compilation, *SMILE, Neoist Music Anthology*, that included two cassettes of selected material from members of the Neoist Web. (I started using the World Wide (Neoist) Web term at around 1980, fifteen years before it would become exploited by the Internet.) At around this time I got introduced to Bill Vorn, member of a popular local band, Rational Youth. With him I produced very melodical, hymnic and mostly traditionally structured pieces, characterized by the use of sequencer, synthesizer, the integration of traditional folk music and pulsating beat. The popular term for this music is electro-pop and later techno-pop. It was a new and mixed field of dance, disco, ambient music and noise, originated by the German group, Kraftwerk. For a while I performed these techno-songs solo, incorporating them into multi-media synthetic-wave performances, Blood Campaign actions, touring in Canada, USA and Europe.

Soon I started founding bands again, from among them the Flaming Neoists and First Aid Brigade. We played in small clubs and big venues, and got contracts for TV shows. But I was more interested in subversive communication networks and Neoism?! than being part of the oily music business. My first two records, *Neoist Songs* and *Mass Media* were released on YUL Records, an independent label in Montreal. Being disappointed with their business orientation and control I felt rather lucky when the label died in '84. Soon I disbanded First Aid Brigade and performed solo, using pre-recorded music. Bill Vorn teamed up with Tristan Renaud and Gaeten Gravel and they produced my tapes.

I moved to New York in '86. There I released *Born Again In Flames* with the help of a very ambitious business man who happened to hear some of my songs and wanted to invest in music. But when he took a closer look at me, he decided to draw back. There was too much anarchy surrounding me and he got scared of the Neoist manifestos I incorporated in my songs. Soon after, in 1988, I produced my only full length album *Ahora Neoismus*. I also released *Demo-Moe's Demolish NYC* LP the same year. Demo-Moe's heavy guitar noise, screaming vocals, free, fucked up drumming is totally different from the sound of my album. By the late 80s I was getting more and more involved with noise. *Ahora Neoismus* still reflects a techno-pop style production but the signs of my changing interest are already there.

In that period of the second half of the 80s I was more concerned about the spreading of Neoism?! than anything else. The impulse to put out a record didn't come from pure musical considerations. The song, as a compact form of text and sound, seemed to be the best material for Neoist propaganda. In the above Scrapmetal stimuli segment I have already mentioned DJ Steve, the great master of scrapmetal music, and I briefly described his style and instruments. For a while he became my close collaborator. I sang Hungarian songs using a megaphone and he played on his metal kit. I exercised my voice (shouting, screaming, yelling, squeaking, etc.) under the noise-friendly environment of Williamsburg Bridge and we practiced together outdoors at the Rivington Garden, Lower East Side. This work has been almost immediately expanded into a group, Hungarian Folk Music, and we played many gigs in New York and toured in Canada. Krista Goddess and Michael Zwicky joined us a few times. I've recorded most of our rehearsals and public performances with my professional Sony Walkman.

The megaphone became my main sound instrument (see Megaphonic convulsions segment) and I also started making my own primitive scrapmetal instruments, junk machines, noise making devices (see Scrapmetal stimuli and Armature/Accumulations segments). Occasionally I worked with co-performers, Gen Ken, Matty Jankowsky, Boy Genius, Brian Damage, Bill Satan, Angela Idealism, Phycus, Ghera, and formed new noise groups in Montreal, New York, Toronto (Nomen Est Omen, Coup d'Etat, Amen, Puppet Government).

By the beginning of the 90s I shifted into a completely new era. Though I hated my new home town, Toronto (I lost my flat in New York, and followed my pregnant girlfriend, Krista, who happened to have a house here). Today, looking at all the shit in my office (see Armature/Accumulation segment), I must admit that this new situation was very productive to develop new ideas and working methods, to explore radical sounds through the making and application of special instruments (kinetic furniture, file cabinets). Many videos and performance videos illustrate this era of sound-based experimentation. When I listen to the recordings I have done since *Ahora Neoismus* and especially during the most recent years, I finally feel less unsatisfied with the results than before (read more about this in Undisciplined crap segment). Though I've put together many different compilations of studio and live recordings, all this stuff (as of 1996) still remains unpublished.

First Aid Brigade, 1982, Montreal, photo curtesy Neoist Archive.
From left to right: Louise Litsz vocals, Monty Cantsin vocals, Jack 5 bass, Josée Carmen vocals, Chico
Luis synth/saxophone, Patrice Roy percussions, Boris Petrowski drums, Jeroen Pichay guitar

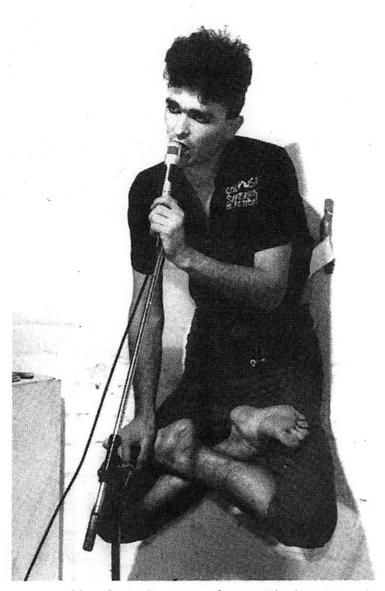

Monty Cantsin, Restriction, performance, Vehicule Art, Montreal

Photo Michel Dubreuil

GIFT TO CHINA – Letter to Ai Weiwei via the AGO
Oct 10, 2013 Toronto

I, the undersigned Istvan Kantor Monty Cantsin?
Amen!, fugitive art criminal, declare, that due to
the intolerable uncertainity of my existence in the
country to which I handed over my body and soul
in 1977, request political and economic asylum
and refugee status in China where artists like me
are taken seriously. Based on mutual sympathy,
love of freedom and passion for art, I take this
opportunity to ask my brother in crime, Ai
Weiwei, to sponsor my formal submission to the
Chinese Embassy in Ottawa. Not having direct
contact with the artist himself I summon the AGO
to intermediate between us and forward this
message to the address where he is currently under
house arrest. To make it authentic and personal, I
sign it with my own blood. It is a work of art. I
attach a signed copy to be added to the AGO's
Istvan Kantor Security Files.

Deeply in debt,

Istvan Kantor Monty Cantsin? Amen
Fugitive art criminal
I REBEL, THEREFORE I AM!

LIBRETTO
LIST OF SCENES

1/ Rebel Poet (RP) walks on the train tracks carrying a couple of pieces of wood planks on his left shoulder. He has a black bag on his head. He collects spikes in a bucket.

2/ Gravedigger (GD) digging in the middle of an empty lot.

3/ RP arrives from the tracks to the site and walks through the ruins.

4/ GD is digging and RP gets behind her and drops the planks.

5/ GD turns to him.
"You came early, I just started digging."

6/ RB pulls of the bag from his head:
"I changed my mind, I don't want to be buried."

7/ GD continues digging.
"I'm digging the grave of your revolution. Your revolution has failed. You have to be buried to rise again."

8/ RP grabs her spade.
"I don't want to be buried. I want to disappear. I want to be crucified and left on the cross to rot. I should be hugged by the wind, washed by the rain, dried by the sun, eaten by the birds and the bugs. Let my flesh slowly perish, only my bones left stuck on the cross until a hurricane pulls the nails out and drops my bones into the ocean."

9/ They get close to each other and fall on the ground, on some corrugated metal and proceed to have an intense sexual interaction.

10/ GD attaches RP with ropes and nails him to the planks with the spikes.

11/ RB is up on the cross, his last words are:
"Don't take me down."

12/ GD is kneeling down and praying in front of the crucifix:
"Nobody will take you down, you'll be left on the cross to rot. You'll be hugged by the wind, washed by the rain, dried by the sun. You'll be eaten by the birds and the bugs. Your flesh will slowly perish, only your bones will be left stuck on the cross until a hurricane pulls the nails out and drops your bones into the ocean. You'll disappear for ever."

13/ RP appears behind GD, bloody, expired.
"I changed my mind. I want to be buried. I want to rise again."

14/ GD bursts into hysterical laugh.

LOOPMACHINE SONG

I REPEAT I REPEAT I REPEAT I REPEAT
I REPEAT I REPEAT I REPEAT I REPEAT
I REPEAT I REPEAT I REPEAT I REPEAT
I AM ISTVAN I AM ISTVAN I AM ISTVAN
I AM ISTVAN I AM ISTVAN I AM ISTVAN
I AM ISTVAN I AM ISTVAN I AM ISTVAN
I AM ISTVAN I AM ISTVAN I AM ISTVAN
I AM ISTVAN I AM ISTVAN I AM ISTVAN
I AM ISTVAN I AM ISTVAN I AM ISTVAN
I AM ISTVAN I AM ISTVAN I AM ISTVAN
I REPEAT I REPEAT I REPEAT I REPEAT
I REPEAT I REPEAT I REPEAT I REPEAT
I REPEAT I REPEAT I REPEAT I REPEAT
I AM I AM I AM I AM I AM I AM I AM
I AM I AM I AM I AM I AM I AM I AM
I AM THE ENEMY

I'M TELLING YOU I'M TELLING YOU
I'M TELLING YOU I'M TELLING YOU
I'M TELLING YOU I'M TELLING YOU
I'M TELLING YOU I'M TELLING YOU
I'M TELLING YOU I'M TELLING YOU
I'M TELLING YOU I'M TELLING YOU
OVER AND OVER
AND OVER AND OVER
AND OVER AND OVER AND OVER
AGAIN AGAIN AGIAN AGAIN AGAIN AGAIN
I'M TELLING YOU OVER AND OVER AND OVER AGAIN
I'M TELLING YOU OVER AND OVER AND OVER AGAIN
I'M TELLING YOU OVER AND OVER AND OVER AGAIN
I'M TELLING YOU OVER AND OVER AND OVER AGAIN
I'M TELLING YOU OVER AND OVER AND OVER AGAIN

I'M TELLING YOU OVER AND OVER AND OVER AGAIN
I'M TELLING YOU I'M TELLING YOU
I'M TELLING YOU I'M TELLING YOU
I'M TELLING YOU I'M TELLING YOU
I'M TELLING YOU I'M TELLING YOU
I'M TELLING YOU I'M TELLING YOU
I'M TELLING YOU I'M TELLING YOU
I'M TELLING YOU I'M TELLING YOU
I'M TELLING YOU I'M TELLING YOU
I'M TELLING YOU I'M TELLING YOU
I'M TELLING YOU I'M TELLING YOU
I'M TELLING YOU
I HAVE NOTHING I HAVE NOTHING
I HAVE NOTHING I HAVE NOTHING
I HAVE NOTHING I HAVE NOTHING
I HAVE NOTHING I HAVE NOTHING
I HAVE NOTHING I HAVE NOTHING
I HAVE NOTHING I HAVE NOTHING
I HAVE NOTHING I HAVE NOTHING
I HAVE NOTHING I HAVE NOTHING
NOTHING NOTHING NOTHING NOTHING NOTHING
NOTHING NOTHING NOTHING NOTHING NOTHING
NOTHING NOTHING NOTHING NOTHING NOTHING
I HAVE NOTHING
I HAVE NOTHING
I HAVE NOTHING
I HAVE NOTHING
I HAVE NOTHING
I HAVE NOTHING
I HAVE NOTHING
I HAVE NOTHING
I HAVE NOTHING
I HAVE NOTHING
I HAVE NOTHING
I HAVE NOTHING
I HAVE NOTHING TO SAY

I'M SICK I'M SICK I'M SICK I'M SICK
I'M SICK I'M SICK I'M SICK I'M SICK
I'M SICK I'M SICK I'M SICK I'M SICK
I'M SICK ABOUT BEING
I'M SICK ABOUT BEING
I'M SICK ABOUT BEING
SICK ABOUT BEING
I'M SICK ABOUT BEING
SICK ABOUT BEING
I'M FED UP I'M FED UP
FED UP FED UP FED UP FED UP
FED UP FED UP FED UP FED UP
I'M FED UP WITH FEEDING
I'M SICK ABOUT BEING
SICK ABOUT BEING
I'M FED UP WITH FEEDING
HOPELESS HOPELESS HOPELESS
HOPELESS HOPELESS HOPELESS
HOPELESS HOPELESS
HOPELESS HOPES

IT HAS IT HAS IT HAS IT HAS
IT HAS IT HAS IT HAS IT HAS
IT HAS BEEN IT HAS BEEN
IT HAS BEEN IT HAS BEEN
IT HAS BEEN IT HAS BEEN
IT HAS BEEN IT HAS BEEN
IT HAS BEEN GOING ON
IT HAS BEEN GOING ON
IT HAS BEEN GOING ON
IT HAS BEEN GOING ON
IT HAS BEEN GOING ON
IT HAS BEEN GOING ON
IT HAS BEEN GOING ON
IT HAS BEEN GOING ON
IT HAS BEEN GOING ON
IT HAS BEEN GOING ON
IT HAS BEEN GOING ON

IT HAS BEEN GOING ON TOO LONG
IT HAS BEEN GOING ON TOO LONG
IT HAS BEEN GOING ON TOO LONG
IT HAS BEEN GOING ON TOO LONG
IT HAS BEEN GOING ON TOO LONG
IT HAS BEEN GOING ON TOO LONG
IT HAS BEEN GOING ON TOO LONG
IT HAS BEEN GOING ON TOO LONG
IT HAS BEEN GOING ON TOO LONG
IT HAS BEEN GOING ON TOO LONG
IT HAS BEEN GOING ON TOO LONG
IT HAS BEEN GOING ON TOO LONG
IT HAS BEEN GOING ON TOO LONG
IT HAS BEEN GOING ON TOO LONG
IT HAS BEEN GOING ON TOO LONG

I JUST WANT TO FUCK I JUST WANT TO FUCK
I JUST WANT TO FUCK I JUST WANT TO FUCK
FUCK FUCK FUCK FUCK FUCK MY BRAINS OUT
FUCK MY BRAINS OUT FUCK MY BRAINS OUT
FUCK MY BRAINS OUT FUCK MY BRAINS OUT
AND DESTROY AND DESTROY
AND DESTROY AND DESTROY
DESTROY DESTROY
DESTROY DESTROY
DESTROY THE WORLD
DESTROY THE WORLD
DESTROY THE WORLD
DESTROY THE WORLD
WITH AN ORGASM WITH AN ORGASM
WITH AN ORGASM WITH AN ORGASM
ORGASM ORGASM ORGASM ORGASM
DESTROY THE WORLD WITH AN ORGASM
I JUST WANT TO FUCK MY BRAINS OUT
AND DESTROY THE WORLD WITH AN ORGASM

At Merapi volcano after eruption, Indonesia, 2011

WORKING TITLE OF PROJECT: DISASTER -

UNUSUALLY HIGH ENVIRONMENTAL DEVASTATIONS have struck Indonesia throughout the past decades including earthquakes, landslides, tsunamis, volcanic activities, fires and floods. The agonizing, shocking sites of these disastrous events, which I have seen only in the media, have left deep marks in my mind and continue to trigger my imagination.

There is a very strong symbolical analogue between the explosive reality of an erupting volcano and an uprising caused by accumulating social fury. Revolutionary filmmaker Guy Debord spent the last two decades of his life at a mountain site in France in order to enjoy surveying the devastating, constant storms surrounding his living space.

My work is known for its strong intellectual relations to social conflicts, riots and revolutions.

My fascination with unrest and disorder originates from my childhood.

Being a post-war child who also lived through revolutions and dictatorships in Eastern Europe, my artistic vision was strongly determined by scenes of ruins, destruction, blood, fire, mayhem and death caused by clashing military forces and oppressed masses of people.

I have been invited to take part in *a residency project* organized by an artist-run centre, 'Performance Klub', located in *Yogyakarta, Indonesia*. During an intellectually and spiritually liberating journey, as part of this residency project, I'll develop a new video work that will explore the subject of "disaster" fuelled and contoured by the local reality. My two months' residency will end with the production of a new video assisted by Performance Klub and participating local artists.

As a multidisciplinary artist working in the fields of visual and media arts, including video, sound, performance and new media, my practice can be described as synergetic and interactive. I create works that are difficult to define because they fuse various disciplines.

Elements of performance documentations are re-formed into a video work which may then turn into a performative part of an installation piece, a manifesto or a simple postcard. My work is open-formed, inviting the viewer to knit disparate components together. In recent years my practice has incorporated street art, public interventions, family revisitations, socio-political actions.

I'm very fortunate to be able to have a network already in place in Indonesia via Performance Klub, the sponsoring organization, and in particular, performance artist Iwan Wijono. Performance Klub is located in Yogyakarta, one of the largest cities in Indonesia which has been particularly hard hit by an earthquake in 2006. The disaster forced the group to reconsider its urban-only policies and re-centre their efforts in the countryside, as well as extending established art making activities with creative assistance to those under urgent need including the provision of food, water, medicines and housing.

Iwan has invited me to participate in a group-oriented, collaborative and process-based art making, outside of the city, involving many of the hundreds who are still living in temporary shelters built of provisional materials. These scenes and materials will be the building blocks for our newly initiated collective work involving the real victims of disasters.

Iwan has seen my work on several occasions and was drawn to its socio-political aspects and community related values. He suggested that I extend my art explorations by investigating the reality of gentrification and housing advocacy, which I have previously addressed in video works like *Broadcast* (2000), *Lebensraum/Lifespace* (2004) and *(The Never Ending) Operetta* (2008). The devastating force of gentrification that hit Toronto twenty years ago somehow resonates through the tragic housing situation after the tsunami struck Indonesia in 2004.

My relationship to the surrounding society and environment has always played an essential role in creating new works. My projects are mostly determined by life events, everyday activities and living space. Exploring the city's architecture in relationship to the results of gentrification is only one example. The *cross-fertilization practice* which I've established with my work in the past is something to be re-explored in the present as part of a revitalizing idea for creative co-operation. That's what I expect from the entire experience in Indonesia. This will include the culture, the people and the places I'll visit and the contacts I'll make. All of these experiences will be captured also on video.

After meeting with villagers through a series of workshops and screenings, I will work together with Iwan Wijono and Performance Klub to realize a post-tsunami/earthquake performance feeding from real events, documentations and memories. It will include spoken word testimonies, pamphlets, flyers, collective and individual explorations of the body, movements, songs, music (sampled and re-orchestrated, and live) as well as videos produced in Indonesia. My experience will be defined by my activist engagement, technical skills and unique working methods, a real life experience/production where everything that is captured will be included in a script and fully explored afterwards according to necessity. I also hope that sudden and unexpected events will occur during my residency which will force me to react to them with speed and efficiency. I expect that my direct interaction with Indonesian culture, nature and society will serve to greatly revitalize my experimental work as a media/performance artist.

I have lived in Montreal, New York, Paris, Budapest, Berlin and Toronto. Changing living spaces has always been extremely important for me as it took my work in different directions under various conditions and circumstances. All the practical and theoretical knowledge I have accumulated during the past decades will serve as an activating force and theoretical device that can be employed in any situation. Each city is a human-controlled living machinery for producing subjectivities, intensities, flows, desires, hopes and circulation/exchange of intellectual nourishment and existential stimulation.

During the past few years I have had the chance to explore different cultural territories such as Japan and Thailand. These short experiences served to bring important results and have greatly increased my interest to do more research in Asian countries. Unfortunately, in these cases, my work was restricted due to insufficient time and lack of partnerships/connections.

The invitation from Performance Klub and Iwan Wijono is exactly what I have been seeking for the real undertaking of a residency. I feel strongly that I must seize this opportunity in order to take a large step forward to accomplish my long nurtured creative goals.

One of my last residencies took place in Berlin, Germany at the Podewil Centre for Contemporary Art, from Aug/2004 to February/2005. The result was the creation of a new robotic installation that was presented at the Art Gallery of York University in 2005, curated by Philip Monk. This work could have not been done anywhere other than in Berlin, where the accumulation of history has a fascinating and crucial impact on everyday life. My most recent residency (one month) was located in ComPeung, an artist community North of Chiang Mai, Thailand, in 2007. This short period resulted in another mind opening experience which was summed up in one of my latest video productions, *White Boy from the East* (2009).

Iwan Wijono is an internationally known performance artist, whom I have met several times at performance art festivals. He suggested to me a few years ago that we could do some work together in collaboration with his organization, Performance Klub, in Yogyakarta.

My plan is to start my residency in Yogyakarta in late December/2010, or early January, 2011. The initial research period will be two weeks followed by the preparation and production of the project. A detailed work plan will be outlined after my arrival in Indonesia with the assistance of Performance Klub and Iwan, and in relationship to realistic working conditions. The residency will end by the end of February/2011 but my work will continue after my return to Toronto with video post-production and distribution. I'll select and re-edit the produced material and put it into a final form. This work will then be circulated at international media art festivals and performance art events as well as at educational institutions. Lastly and most importantly it's necessary to repeat that art is a communication device that connects people, places and ideas in order to increase the realization of creativity for the benefit of everyone. Stop misery!

Hanging at a rescue centre, Merapi area, Indonesia, 2011

HISTORY WILL ABSOLVE ME

As a result of so many turbid and illegal machinations, due to the will of those who govern and the weakness of those who judge, I find myself here in this freight elevator at the National Gallery, where I have been brought to be tried in secret, so that I may not be heard and my voice may be stifled, and so that no one may learn of the things I am going to say. Why such interest in silencing me? Are they that afraid of the truth? When this speech is over, I do not want to have to reproach myself for any principle left undefended, for any truth left unsaid, for any authority not denounced. I want to clear the field for an assault against all the endless lies and deceits, the hypocrisy, conventionalism and moral cowardice that have set the stage for this crude comedy. I warn you, I am just beginning! If there is in your hearts a vestige of love for art, love for humanity, love for justice, listen carefully. I know that I will be silenced for many years; I know that the art system will try to suppress the truth by all possible means; I know that there will be a conspiracy to bury me in oblivion. But my voice will not be stifled—it will rise from my breast even when I feel most alone, and my heart will give it all the fire that callous cowards deny. I carry the teachings of revolutionaries in my heart, and in my mind the noble ideas of all true artists who have defended people's freedom everywhere!

The fact is, when artists carry the same ideals in their hearts, nothing can isolate them—neither prison walls nor the grass of cemeteries. For a single memory, a single spirit, a single idea, a single conscience, a single dignity will sustain them all. I am not obliged to keep my ideals secret, for I am bound only by the truth. How to keep secret what is really happening, when so many young artists are willing to risk everything—prison, torture and death, if necessary—in order that the truth be told.

After depriving me of everything else, they finally deprived me even entry to my own home where creativity lives. It was evident that a whole system of institutional terror shrank in fear of the moral conviction of a defenceless person—unarmed, slandered and isolated.

What unbelievable crimes this system must have committed to so fear the voice of one single artist!

I want to speak of the goals that inspired us in our struggle:

To totally discredit the cowardly, miserable and treacherous lies which the corporate system had hurled against us; to reveal with irrefutable evidence the horrible, repulsive crimes the authoritarian institutions had practiced on the prisoner-artists; and to show the nation and the world the infinite misfortune of the creative people who are suffering the cruelest, the most inhuman oppression of their history. Artists are made of flesh and blood; they think, observe, feel. They are susceptible to the opinions, beliefs, sympathies and antipathies of the people. If you ask their opinion, they may tell you they cannot express it in words; but that does not mean they have no opinion. They are affected by exactly the same problems that affect other citizens— subsistence, rent, the education of their children, their future, etc. Everything of this kind is an inevitable point of contact between them and the people and everything of this kind relates them to the past, present and future situation of the society in which they live. With what right do the museums send to prison artists who have tried to redeem the system of art by giving their own blood, their own lives? All this is monstrous to the eyes of the people and to the principles of justice! The right of rebellion against tyranny, Honourable Judges, has been recognized from the most ancient times to the present day by people of all creeds, ideas and doctrines.

I call you to abandon the odious flag of institutional tyranny and to embrace the banner of freedom.

Now that the truth is coming out, now that speaking before you I am carrying out the mission I set for myself, I may die peacefully and content. Condemn me. It does not matter. It's always 6 o'clock. History will absolve me.

Based on a speech given by Fidel Castro in 1953.

NEOIST STANZA

When I fuck
I think about NEOISM?!,
when I eat
I think about NEOISM?!,
when I walk
I think about NEOISM?!,
when I take a shit
I think about NEOISM?!,
when I look at my bills
I think about NEOISM?!,
when I get arrested
I think about NEOISM?!,
when I turn off the light
I think about NEOISM?!,
in the dark
I think about NEOISM?!,
when I masturbate
I think about NEOISM?!,
when I go to the bank
I think about NEOISM?!,
when the telephone rings
I think about NEOISM?!,
when I loose my temper
I think about NEOISM?!,
when I watch tv
I think about NEOISM?!,
when I read the papers
I think about NEOISM?!,
when I sleep
I think about NEOISM?!,
when I'm sick
I think about NEOISM?!,

when I'm in love
I think about NEOISM?!,
when I take a picture
I think about NEOISM?!,
when I set things on fire
I think about NEOISM?!,
when I iron my shirt
I think about NEOISM?!,
when it's cold
I think about NEOISM?!,
when the summer comes
I think about NEOISM?!,
when someone dies
I think about NEOISM?!,
when a baby cries
I think about NEOISM?!,
when a war starts
I think about NEOISM?!,
when people are happy
I think about NEOISM?!,
when I have to pay
I think about NEOISM?!,
when I listen to music
I think about NEOISM?!,
when my body gets hot
I think about NEOISM?!,
when I spit
I think about NEOISM?!,
when look out the window
I think about NEOISM?!,
when I play with the kids
I think about NEOISM?!,
in the doctor's office
I think about NEOISM?!,

at the police station
I think about NEOISM?!,

sitting on a train
I think about NEOISM?!,
getting a blow job
I think about NEOISM?!,
reading Lenin
I think about NEOISM?!,
running from my enemies
I think about NEOISM?!,
looking at the sky
I think about NEOISM?!,
drinking water
I think about NEOISM?!,
when I wash my hands
I think about NEOISM?!,
in the kitchen
I think about NEOISM?!,
cleaning a fish
I think about NEOISM?!,
opening oysters
I think about NEOISM?!,
painting the walls
I think about NEOISM?!,
reading Mao's biography
I think about NEOISM?!,
when I hug Ceres
I think about NEOISM?!,
when I break a chair
I think about NEOISM?!,
when I wash the floor
I think about NEOISM?!,
when I see my blood
I think about NEOISM?!,
when I hear the sirens
I think about NEOISM?!,
when I read the bible
I think about NEOISM?!,
when I get high

I think about NEOISM?!,
when I cant find something
I think about NEOISM?!,
when the train comes
I think about NEOISM?!,
when a bomb explodes
I think about NEOISM?!,
before I die
I'll think about NEOISM?!,
when I won't think about NEOISM?!
I'll be dead

Restriction, Vehicle Art, Montreal, 1980

Photo: Michel Dubreuil

BLOOD AND RUINS

(Istvan Kantor) Monty Cantsin? Amen. interviewed by Lucy Ditti, oct/1993

Before meeting with Istvan Kantor/Monty Cantsin, most recently also known as AMEN. (Amen Dot), I recollected my memories of the performances I saw him doing since I met him for the first time for a radio interview somewhere in 1980. I saw him hanging on the wall at Vehicule Art, like a punk Hindu god, blood running down on his face and singing the anthem of total freedom. I watched him through a transparent curtain, he was naked, sitting on the toilet, eating mushrooms and typing (I heard only later that he was typing the same phrase "no performance pas" for the duration of the two week event), in his own apartment on rue Cartier that was then the central headquarters of the First Neoist Apartment Festival, with participants from Europe, USA, Canada. I saw him at Café Campus, leading a gang of leather jacket bikers into the packed room while his collaborators were terrifying the audience with flaming irons. I saw him encircled by video technology and talking to his own magnetic copy about his theory of Neoism. I saw him singing to his white rats, wearing a huge carp (yes, the fish) on his head, accompanied by his pop band, First Aid Brigade, at the Spectrum, in 1983. I was there when he made a blood painting on the white ballerina outfit of his girlfriend at Club Soda, and a few years later I saw him splashing his blood on the naked body of his pregnant wife in front of the guests of the opening of his mini-retrospective "THE BEST SHIT OF MY WORST YEARS," at Espace Global. I saw him in front of Dutchy's, in the street, performing songs from his latest album, setting fire on different objects, asking people to join his movement if they want to be immortal. This year I saw Cantsin at the opening of Les Cent jours, kneeling in front of his blood stained monument, posing like a beggar, holding a gold turd on his palm.

These are only a few examples of his local performances from the past fifteen years. He also toured extensively in Europe, from Berlin to Paris via München, Prague, Belgrade, Budapest, he performed everywhere in North America, from New York to San Francisco via Quebec, Toronto, Winnipeg, Calgary, Vancouver, and, through his videos, he has been seen all over the world. Kantor has never been into the trip of post-modern sleeping pills. Besides performances and videos, he also produced several albums in the 80s, pioneering new techno sound, writing manifestos and spreading Neoist propaganda. He always pushed things to the extremes. While other artists crossed over to more accessible forms, he chose the risky business of cultural subversion. He has been arrested, censured, put in prison, evicted, banned.

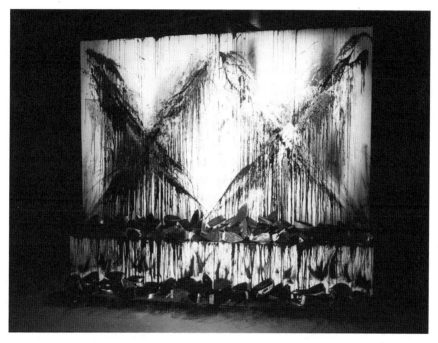

XX-Monument Temporaire, installation, 1993

Lucy Ditti: For a long time you have been Montreal's most feared performer, you have been the centre of scandals for drinking your own blood or making blood paintings, using animals on stage, terrorizing galleries and museums, making assaulting videos, being an anti-art artist. But in the past recent years you haven't been seen much in Montreal. We heard from you again this summer when "Les Cent jours d'art contemporain" opened, including a sculptural installation of your work "XX-Monument Temporaire."

Istvan Kantor: Let's face it, for many years you didn't even want to hear about me. In the late seventies people didn't mind to give their energy for an unknown cause. We wanted to do something new. And we kept searching for it instead of turning it over to the market. We did what we had to do. But the short period of local cultural rebellion was over by the mid eighties. Montreal has been taken by the enemy. The places where we used to do our stuff are all dead now. The yuppies cleaned the way for the Hollywood-avant-garde and pseudo-punk fashion mongers to cross over to show business. In this situation I have been forced to give up my activities here.

L.D.: You moved your headquarters to New York for a while, to continue your world wide conspiracy and to get new energy and fresh inspiration. You refused to let yourself down by the oppressive circumstances, and rather used it as an impulse for a change.

I.K.: I went to New York, but I lived in the Lower East Side. It's very different from any other parts of New York or America. The Lower East Side was the only place where someone like me, an illegal alien with revolutionary ambitions, could survive. It was the only place where people accepted me for what I am and also encouraged me to do what I wanted to do. I could focus on my ideas and I got constant inspiration from the people of my neighbourhood.

L.D.: An accomplished master of propaganda/publicity, and someone who knows well that self-promotion is the secret of survival, you started your publicity campaign by using a giant ghetto blaster and a megaphone and performed your songs and speeches at street corners, distributed pamphlets to passers-by, and your posters, stickers and graffiti were seen everywhere.

I.K.: I trained enough in Montreal. We (the Neoists) used to be the best in covering the whole city with posters and graffiti. We got arrested night after night until we learned that the best time for postering was very early morning when the cops were drinking their coffee.

L.D.: As a result of your Neoist campaign, you almost immediately became known in New York as Monty Cantsin "The Self-appointed Leader of the People of the Lower East Side." You performed at all of the newly opened, now already almost legendary places, like the Gas Station, No Se No, Rivington School Garden, Generator. And your MOMA blood-X action in 1988 turned you into a media star.

I.K.: The local media in New York were always closely following my activities, without me making much efforts. Today in Montreal no journalist will go to an underground event, not even from the so called alternative press anymore, if you don't have a full page ad in the papers and you are not promoted by a well known institution or agency at least three weeks prior to the event. In New York when I first performed at the Gas Station the place was yet totally unknown, we only gave away a couple of hundred flyers the day before but I've got reviewed in the *Village Voice*, in *Downtown* mag, etc. So it was very normal that the MOMA action made all the newspapers. It was an international event, a protest against police brutality and institutional dictatorship, a radical socio-cultural-critical action that involved many actual political issues. There is no reason to praise the media for being what the media should be. The job of the media is to give information to people.

L.D.: Your installation at Les Cent jours is an occasion to present your new work to a larger public in Montreal. A selection of your videos (four hours of material selected to fit the theme of his installation) was also shown at the Cinema Parallel. But you say this has nothing to do with a new recognition of your work.

I.K.: Claude Gosselin, director of Les Cent jours, knows me and my work since the late seventies. In fact he is really the only one doing something that connects the large public to living art. He always defended my work in the past but he never took the risk to directly manifest his interest in my ideas. I believe he paid a long time debt when he finally invited me this year.

L.D.: I saw your non-official intervention at the opening of Les Cent jours in 1987, when you and your Neoist collaborators juried the works by holding up numbers, from 0 to 10, but there were always more zeros than other numbers.

I.K.: Yes, I am critical and like to create critical situations. But that "Jury" performance was also very ironic, a mockery of art openings. I always have problems with organizers and institutions wherever I go and it was never easy to deal with Claude either, but this year we finally have done something substantial. Money was a crucial part of the process because I've got a mini-budget for this installation. But the most interesting is the ignorance of the critics. In the reviews about Les Cent jours published in Canadian art magazines, my name has never been mentioned. And the worst is that I actually like that. When I'm neglected I feel stronger because I know I have done something meaningful. My inspiration comes through restriction, from humiliating conditions, from misery. Today it's really fashionable to be an angry artist, and so I try to grow out of it, but the fact is that I can't, because for me it's not just a trendy attitude but my own character.

The Jury, Neoist group, Les Cent jours, 1987

L.D.: In a performance/conference, planned for the last day of Les Cent jours, oct 31, you will explain your work in general as well as talk about the subject of this installation.

I.K.: A couple of years ago, when I wanted to give a talk at the National Gallery in Ottawa, I was immediately arrested and put in jail. While the security guards were forcing me out of the Marcel Duchamp room I was screaming: "Let me talk, I want to talk." But I couldn't say much more. I was pushed into an elevator and I had to remain there until the police took me to the city prison. Now I've got a chance to say what I want. The greatest works of art were always insulting, irritating, or at least they were questioning established rules. The greatest artists always vandalized the notion of art. I have never really thought about vandalism until I read it in a newspaper that what I was doing is vandalism. For many years I tried to defend myself against this accusation. I always used empty white walls to make my blood paintings and if some drops fell on a Picasso, like for example at the Museum of Modern Art, it was not my intention. My intention was to give a gift to the museum. I always asked them to keep it until it becomes meaningless, obsolete. Of course they never accepted my donations, and they quickly eliminated my works, washed and painted the walls, cleaned the floors. Should I say that by cleaning up the gallery they vandalized my work? That would give them too much credit. Anyway, after a while I realized that the best is to admit their accusation of vandalism without being afraid of this term. So I decided that I should not defend myself against vandalism but I should defend vandalism as the ultimate act of creation, and that's the basic idea of this exhibition.

L.D.: Presently you live in Montreal and in Toronto.

I.K.: I had to leave New York in '91, being kicked out from my studio by a new landlord who wanted to turn the place into a better paying doctor's office. I had enough other problems with authorities and, instead of taking up the fight with the much hated gentrification process, I moved my studio to Toronto. I always resist as long as I can. But my girlfriend was pregnant then and she was from Toronto so the best solution seemed to be to move again and start a new mission in a new city. But as you know, I always kept a room in Montreal for my works, for my archives, and because, in spite of all, I like this city and I want to spend time here.

Last year the city evicted me from my Outremont apartment, my headquarters for a decade, because of the landlord's accusation of satanist-blood-rituals, sex orgies and racist hooliganism. The landlord, a member of a religious community, didn't have much respect for new artistic experimentation.

L.D.: Now you rent a secret studio in Ville-Émard, far from downtown but close to the industrial zone.

I.K.: Ville-Émard is like living in Williamsburg (of New York). I like the architecture, the Canal, the old restaurants, the low rent and the people. The biggest scrapyard of the Montreal area is five minutes from my studio. A great place to collect material and to listen to scrapmetal music.

L.D.: During the past 20 years you have lost lots of blood on the barricades and yet you are not interested in changing your life style and ideas. To mark the end of your installation you are planning to eliminate the exhibited works, demolish your monument, scrap everything.

I.K.: I made them for this installation, for the duration of Les Cent jours. Time is part of every work of art. Artworks have two basic values: the ideal value and the market value. A blood painting that gets almost immediately destroyed after its making has only one value: ideal value, the message is given, the work is eliminated, that's it. Otherwise if we keep an artwork for an unlimited time it will soon lose its ideal value and its meaning will be that of its market value. An $82-million Van Gogh means nothing else than $82 million. Duchamp said that fifty years is the maximum life of an artwork. I've got only 100 days for this installation.

L.D.: While most artists are eager to be included in museum collections because that's the way artists get recognition, and get immortalized in a small or larger room, you say that it is much more difficult not to be included in a museum. All of your unwanted blood works were destroyed by the very dramatic circumstances of their making and by the conflicts with museum officials. Now you want to do it yourself. It seems like you want to make sure that these works will never be exhibited in museums.

I.K.: I'm not trying to destroy art, it has been done by the art market. Artists are making art because that's the only way they can live, survive, but their work is being used against them to promote the art market. I'm trying to bring art back to life, raise it from the dead, make it part of our life again, reanimate it, yes, that's what I really want to do. I'm not wasting my blood for nothing. I'm using extreme situations to trigger a very strong reaction, to exactly define my theory and practice. I have to create a crisis in order to present the cause. The blood-X marks the nerve centre of this crisis around which circulates people's opinion, the reality of laws, politics, spirituality, sexuality, and they intertwine to create a chaotic, convulsive and somewhat coherent pattern. That's my working method. I don't mind being called a criminal; in fact, I believe that to become an artist first you have to become a criminal.

Istvan Kantor will talk and perform on oct 31st, 1993, 3pm, at Les Cents jours, corner of ave du Park and Prince Arthur. Bring your chainsaw if you want to help.

THAT'S HOW I WANT TO BE REMEMBERED

Standing on my head
and thinking about NEOISM?!
THAT'S HOW I WANT TO BE REMEMBERED

Taking blood from my arm in vacutainer tubes
while singing the International Anthem of NEOISM?!
THAT'S HOW I WANT TO BE REMEMBERED

Sticking a blood tube into my asshole in Halasana position
while explaining the Spider Web Strategy of NEOISM?!
THAT'S HOW I WANT TO BE REMEMBERED

Holding up a flaming iron and dancing to the beat of NEOISM?!
THAT'S HOW I WANT TO BE REMEMBERED

Sitting on a NEOIST?! Chair and distributing leaflets to passers-by
THAT'S HOW I WANT TO BE REMEMBERED

Masturbating and watching myself on a video monitor while
thinking about everything I have done in the name of NEOISM?!
THAT'S HOW I WANT TO BE REMEMBERED

Reading from The Book of NEOISM?! to my children at bedtime
THAT'S HOW I WANT TO BE REMEMBERED

Fucking a file cabinet at Addmore Furniture during a performance event
exploring information machinery, office furniture music and NEOISM?!
THAT'S HOW I WANT TO BE REMEMBERED

Eating oysters, drinking champaign, making jokes about sex and
NEOISM?!
while having bubble-bath Sunday morning with my lover
THAT'S HOW I WANT TO BE REMEMBERED

Surrounded by security in front of a bloody wall in a museum
and repeating the same phrase like a maniac:
I did it for NEOISM?!, I did it for NEOISM?!
THAT'S HOW I WANT TO BE REMEMBERED

Staring into a camera at the very instant when my head
suddenly explodes being hit by a seemingly harmless
but mindblowing definition of NEOISM?!
THAT'S HOW I WANT TO BE REMEMBERED

Immortal Gift, Hamburger Bahnhof, Berlin, 2004

EPITAPH

Holy Mary and The Revolutionist – script for video

1/ *The Revolutionist* is walking with a stick, in strange lunge like movements in the empty, dead city, over the train tracks, under trees, next to industrial ruins. Stops, looks around, picks up things from the ground and collects them in a bag. His movements are freakish. His head is covered by a black transparent veil and under it he wears a gas mask.

2/ *Holy Mary* is walking around in an abandoned, swamp like field covered with highly grown weeds. She is holding a large book and reading it, like she was practicing a text in whisper. She is also moving slow, balancing herself like she was disabled. She wears a transparent protection shield on her face. Everything suggests that perhaps we are in a post-apocalyptic stage of history, during the Ultimate Global Aftermath inhabited only by disabled robots.

3/ *The Revolutionist* is looking up to the sky like he is waiting for a sign. On his belt buckle an LED sign glows and rolls: "EAT SHIT."

4/ *Holy Mary* is looking around and up, like she is also expecting something or someone, she is mumbling, talks to herself.

5/ *The Revolutionist* suddenly arrives from behind her and taps her shoulder with his stick to stop her.

6/ *Holy Mary* turns around and bursts into laughing excitedly, her voice sounds queer, deviant, puzzling.

7/ *The Revolutionist*: "Stop it please, just lead me there." He also has an peculiar, unfamiliar voice.

8/ *The Revolutionist* follows Holy Mary through the weeds.

9/ "Here it is," says *Holy Mary*, as she points to a pile of scrappy wood.

10/ They are standing at a poorly made construction that is supposed to be a grave but rather looks like a broken coffin. Foam sheets fill the bottom of it covered with spray painted black graffti sings "FUCK THE WORLD" and "PERMANENT DISASTER" over colourful stencils of skulls, birds and bugs.

11/ *The Revolutionist*: "This piece of shit? This is my coffin?!" He takes a break for a second to think and then bursts into loud laughing. "Hahaha …" The he expresses himself verbally. "Excellent! It's beautiful! It's grandiose, monumental, It's glorious, majestic!" He gets more and more excited. "It's my mausoleum. My pyramid! Thank you! I deserve it! I'm a NEOIST, Revolutionist! A fugitive on the run. A false prophet. I am the Self-Appointed Leader of the People of the Lower East Side(s)! …" He stops again … "I don't know who the hell am I … !?

12/ *Holy Mary*: "I know who you are. But this is the end of your journey, honey, you'll be fine in this emergency casket. Let me help you in …"

13/ *The Revolutionist*: "Wait, Holy Mary, wait!" he begs her as he backs up towards the coffin… then stops, and delivers his speech: "I'm a stranger to myself, I don't know who the hell am I. I refuse and deny, refuse and deny! Existence is not a necessity, survival is annihilation. I can guarantee that nothing will turn out all right. Everything will remain just as fucked up as it has always been. No oki, no doki!" His words are a mix of AI language, common sense, appropriations, programmed information, repeats, etc. "I'm tired of being … to hell! I lived for all and I'll die for all. No, no sorrow that it's over, No, no sorrow that it's over, I'm glad it's over, over, over, over, over. I'm speaking here as a prophet today we are born before our time. There is no way, there is no way no way we can survive. I'm tired of being … to hell, long live permanent disaster, I lived for all and I'll die for all, long live permanent rebellion! Where I come from I can no longer say, I come from nowhere, I belong nowhere, I am the slave and the master, I am the king of disaster, Kill me Holy Mary, kill me now and forever, kill me …"

14/ *Holy Mary* pushes him and they both fall into the coffin. They instantly start fucking in jerking, crazy, exaggerated motions like they were rather trying to simulate, mock, imitate sexual intercourse, but make it look like it's real, grabbing each other in very intense, machine-like movements, it's a weird, hasty, mechanical, seemingly never ending improvisational act.

15/ *The Revolutionist* is laying dead in the coffin. *Holy Mary* covers his eyes with strange, thorny looking pieces what could be called "alien shrouds" but they are actually the shells of horse-chestnuts. She also puts a piece of complete horse-chestnut between his lips.

16/ *Holy Mary* performs a funeral speech, she is reading it from the large book she was holding at the beginning. "Nobody knows from where he came from, he refused to have a home. He was controlled and commanded by the spectres of divinities and surrounded by billions of masters. They programmed and ordered him to stay alive and survive all disasters. He got fed up with being made and to serve technological society as a humanoid slave. He damaged his programmed identity and self-inflicted serious injuries in his memory in order to practice the human laws of permanent misery, to experience fear, rebellion and despair. He was fortunate to be excluded from the institutionalized leadership of the establishment and to have never made anyone suffer in the corridors of power. Any gesture for survival cost him more effort than it would cost dictators to establish their draconian rules or guerrilla fighters to overthrow it. His execution was his own decision. He chose to be fucked to death and die as a false prophet to be forgotten for ever. Amen."

17/ *Holy Mary* closes the coffin, puts a plywood top on it. Then she takes the bag *The Revolutionist* carried and empties it on the coffin's top. A big load of horse-chestnuts falls out from the bag on the top of the coffin, making a rumbling, reverberating, drumming noise.

18/ *Holy Mary* is holding up the large book, it's burning on the top with high flames but we can see the title "The Future of the Body."

19/ *Holy Mary* is writing on the gravestone using a black marker: FU(CK)IT as credits roll in.

20/ *The Revolutionist* appears behind her as a ghost, slowly moving towards her. He is holding a toy piano and singing a folk song. The End.

Note: "Scripture", "Libretto" and "Epitaph" compose a video trilogy under the title "The Future of the Body", a work in progress for several years and a collaboration between Istvan Kantor (script/director/performer) and Jake Chirico (cinematography/editing) to be completed by the time this book will be also published, Fall/2023.

The coffin, construction/art Istvan Kantor / photo Sandy Baron

MY HOUSE – LETTER TO MY MOM

(1979)

Dear Anyu,

I only have good news for you.
I stopped daydreaming about becoming
a famous artist, great writer or immortal revolutionary …
I have made a vital decision that I'll build my own house,
brick by brick.

Walking around in my neighbourhood in the east side
of Montreal and thinking about the kind of house
I would like to build, I got really lucky and almost instantly
I found three bricks at the site of a ruined warehouse building,
close to my present apartment.
I picked them up and carried them home
to mark the beginning of construction.

Plus, a couple of days later, I saw an old folding chair, left
in the street. I also took it home envisaging myself
sitting on it in front of my future house.

But for now I put the chair in the middle of the living room,
placed the three bricks on the seat,
and attached a Neoism sign to the back of it.
It's a beautiful sculptural piece now, a composed ready-made
entitled "My House." I can't stop gazing at it!

So please don't worry about me, I'm fine
and very busy planning my future.

Istvan

P.S.: And you can tell to Apu that I'm not angry at him anymore for ripping off my favourite Che Guevara poster from the wall and throwing it in the garbage when I was 17 years old. In fact I found a few really beautiful and large Guevara posters in thrift stores and now they are embellishing the walls in my apartment. I also found a couple of books about his heroic life and tragic death, in both french and english, and now they are my ideal readings to perfect both languages.

Anyu – Mom / Apu – Dad

Photo: Ariane Laezza 2017

Acknowledgements

ThanXXX to all Refugee Artists, Neoist Insurgents, Plunderground Masters, Full-time Runaways, Self-trained Fugitives, Extraterrestrial Outcasts, Revolutionary Stateless Nobodies, Submerging Creators, Heroic Cultural Guerrillas, Experimental Gladiators, Renegade Poets, Street Corner Philosophers, Pioneering Desperados, Art Criminals, Free-Spirited Working-Class Sex-Workers, Anti-Artists, Noise Makers, Data Pirates, Utopian Post-Situ Anarchists, Reality Hackers, SciFi Ambassadors, Spaceship Beggars, Humanoid SciBot Slaves, Doomsday Survivors, Reprogrammed Damaged Replicants, Gravedigger Enthusiasts ...

I owe special thanks to those who tried to stop me in doing things by constantly control-freaking my creative activities throughout my life. Resisting authoritarian power and struggle against dictatorial leaderships remains my principal driving force. Down with the Rentagon! All power to the maggots! Long Live the Spirit of Che Guevara! Neoism Now and Then! In tribute to Márton Kosznovszki, Hungarian cowman.

About the Author

Istvan Kantor became interested in rebellion and radical artistic experiments at a young age, staging clandestine happenings, performances, and exhibitions under a severe Eastern Block dictatorship. Formerly a folk-singer/poet and a medical student, Kantor gave up his university studies at age 26 and fled from Budapest to Paris where he became a subway singer and received political refugee status. A year later, in 1977, he immigrated to Montreal where he initiated Neoism in 1979. Better known under his Neoist "nome de guerre" Monty Cantsin, Kantor/Cantsin lived in New York during the 1980s while also keeping his studio in Montreal, before settling in Toronto in 1991 with his three children. A multidisciplinary artist, his practice includes correspondence art, media art, performance, installation, sound art, robotics, writing, and music. More than a dozen of his biographic novels and collections of essays were published in Canada, USA, Poland, Hungary, Estonia, among them *Amazing Letters— The Life and Art of David Zack* (2010), *Istvan Kantor—Permanent Revolution* (2013), *Media Revolt* (2014), *Rivington School: 80s New York Underground* (2017), *The Book of Neoism?!* (2018), *Hero In Art— The Vanished Traces of Richard Hambleton* (2020), *Neoism—40 Years of Pop-Up Revolution* (2020), *Roll Over Picasso!: E.F. Higgins III—His Life Art Legend* (2023). He has been causing controversy with his illegal blood-interventions since the mid 80s, notably at the Musée d'art contemporain de Montréal (1985), Museum of Modern Art, New York (1988), the National Gallery of Canada, Ottawa (1991), Hamburger Bahnhof, Berlin (1997), The Art Gallery of Ontario, Toronto (2006) and the Whitney Museum of American Art, New York (2014). His video works have been recognized throughout the world, and have been presented at numerous festivals, including Documenta 8 (1987), the International Short Film Festival Oberhausen (1992), WRO '97 Media Art Binennale, Wroczlaw, Poland, Transmediale, Berlin (2001), and European Media Arts Festival, Osnabruck (2009). His robotic installations have received acclaim at the Ars Electronica Festival,

Linz, Austria, WRO Biennale, Wroclaw, Poland, Centre for Art and Media (ZKM), Karlsruhe, Germany, and ELEKTRA, Montreal, and they were the subject of a large retrospective at the Art Gallery of York University, Toronto (2005). He has recorded over a dozen albums of songs, solo and with groups, among them Monty Cantsin, First Aid Brigade, Hungarian Folk Music and Red Armband. In 1998, Kantor received the Telefilm Canada award for best Canadian video, and in 2004 the Governor General's Award for Visual and Media Arts— the highest accolade attributed in Canada to artists in recognition for their life achievements. Istvan Kantor keeps a large archive of his art/documentation/correspondence in Toronto, Canada as well as in Székesfehérvár, Hungary and continues travelling extensively in North America and Europe, and more recently also in Asia, including Japan, Thailand, Indonesia and China.